Praise for

GAME OVER

"Leeb eloquently and methodically lays out why it is time to take giant steps to solve the world's economic problems that have become so overwhelming. The Game may indeed be over, unless the world's population and policy makers recognize and act soon on the gargantuan problems we are facing."

—Gene Marcial, senior writer and
"Inside Wall Street" columnist, *BusinessWeek*

"Leeb again hits the spot! He not only delineates the causes of our current financial tragedy but also cogently argues for an international economic path that may lead governments, private institutions, and individuals through the present breakdown and toward a more welcomed and robust future."

—Nicholas Rockefeller, former vice chairman,
The RockVest Group of Investors

"Dr. Leeb deserves consideration for a prominent role on the president's National Economic Council. By translating troubling global economic problems such as resource competition, the need for alternative energies, and hidden inflationary pressures into solutions for managing our citizens' wealth, Leeb's advice on the national stage would finally put policy makers on the side of the people."

—Dr. Patrick J. DeSouza, CEO, Plain Sight Group,
former director, Inter-American Affairs of the
National Security Council, White House, and
author of *Economic Strategy and National Security*

Getting in on the Ground Floor: How to Make Money Now—And from Now On—In the New Bull Market
by Stephen Leeb and Donna Leeb

Market Timing for the Nineties: The Five Key Signals for When to Buy, Hold, and Sell
by Stephen Leeb and Roger S. Conrad

The Agile Investor: Profiting from the End of Buy and Hold
by Stephen Leeb and Roger Conrad

Defying the Market: Profiting in the Turbulent Post-Technology Market Boom
by Stephen Leeb and Donna Leeb

The Oil Factor: Protect Yourself and Profit from the Coming Energy Crisis
by Stephen Leeb and Donna Leeb

The Coming Economic Collapse: How You Can Thrive When Oil Costs $200 a Barrel
by Stephen Leeb and Glen Strathy

Game Over

How You Can Prosper in a Shattered Economy

Stephen Leeb, PhD,
with Donna Leeb, Glen Strathy,
William Leeb, and Genia Turanova

**BUSINESS
PLUS**

NEW YORK   BOSTON

Business Plus
Hachette Book Group
237 Park Avenue
New York, NY 10017
Visit our Web site at www.HachetteBookGroup.com.

Business Plus is an imprint of Grand Central Publishing.
The Business Plus name and logo are trademarks of Hachette Book Group, Inc.

Originally published in hardcover by Business Plus.

Printed in the United States of America

First International Trade Edition: January 2009

10 9 8 7 6 5 4 3 2 1

ISBN 978-0-446-54510-5

To Tim
May all your dreams come true

Contents

Author's Note   ix

Introduction   1

PART I
RESOURCE SHORTAGES: FACING FACTS   11

Chapter 1. Oil: Racing to Run-Out   13

Chapter 2. Vicious Circles: Oil, Metals, and Minerals   25

Chapter 3. Water Is a Commodity, Too   34

Chapter 4. The Developing World   43

Chapter 5. The Curse and Cost of Complexity   58

Chapter 6. Wall Street, Complexity, and the
            Shortfall in Resources   68

PART II
MEETING THE CHALLENGE   77

Chapter 7. We Never Said It Would Be Easy   79

Chapter 8. Alternative Energies   86

Chapter 9. More on Alternative Energies   100

Chapter 10. Buying Time   113

Chapter 11. Denial and Disaster   124

PART III
ECONOMIC TSUNAMI 135

Chapter 12. The Inflation Bomb   137

Chapter 13. Inflation: Why the Old Solutions Will
             No Longer Work   149

PART IV
INVESTMENTS FOR A CHAOTIC WORLD 165

Chapter 14. Gold: Your Single Best Bet as the
             Commodity Crisis Unfolds   167

Chapter 15. BRAC: Staying Afloat by Investing Abroad   189

Chapter 16. Investing in the New Resource War   205

Chapter 17. Investing in the Solutions   213

Chapter 18. Our Best Hope: A Flatter World After All   222

Index   233

Acknowledgments   243

About the Author   245

Author's Note

Talk about timing. As this book left our hands to enter production, the United States was embarking upon a financial meltdown that in a matter of days has irrevocably altered Wall Street's landscape. The near failure and last-minute rescue of Bear Stearns; the virtual nationalization of Fannie Mae and Freddie Mac; the demise of Lehman Brothers; the near failure and rescue of AIG; the $750 billion federal bailout of the financial industry, the massive drop in both stocks and commodities, and more—these are all extraordinary events whose full repercussions have yet to unfold. And we have no doubt that further changes lie ahead.

Against this rapidly evolving backdrop, is our book still relevant to investors? Could *any* investment book be relevant?

You bet. Here's why we'd change barely a word of what follows, other than, if we could, reference recent events as further evidence for many of our key arguments relating to the turbulent outlook for the economy and investors that we have projected.

First, while at the moment the turmoil among financial institutions is on center stage, the underlying realities that impelled us to write this book in the first place remain as true, as urgent to confront, and as pertinent to investors as ever—and, dangerously, they are being ignored. The vicious circles we describe that link oil and other commodities won't disappear. The need to develop alternative energies on a large scale *before it becomes impossible to do so* remains utterly pressing. Civilization's very survival remains at stake, and it would be tragic if the dramatic events in the financial arena distract us any further from tackling these basic and critical issues.

Second, a chief implication of these underlying realities—the prospects for ongoing economic turbulence that ultimately will skew ever more toward rising and ultrahigh inflation—holds even truer now than previously as financial institutions founder and the government is taking on massive new obligations. For investors, it has become more important than ever to understand the nature of the economic tsunami we face.

In particular, it's essential to realize that the sharp fall in commodities is a temporary reprieve that is sowing the seeds of its own demise. The reason is that when commodity prices drop, critical new projects get shut down because prices aren't high enough to make them profitable. Eventually, however, demand for commodities is certain to rise as the unprecedented injections of money into the economy bring growth back—to a world where commodities are in even shorter supply than they would have been had prices not dropped. The result will be a rapid and steep rebound in prices.

In other words, the recent extraordinary events demonstrate, as we explain in the following pages, that the world is ineluctably trapped between flirtations with deflation and ever higher inflation.

Third, against this background, the investments we urge you to buy are even more essential than just a few weeks back. And the risks of investing unwisely have become concomitantly greater.

Fourth, the current meltdown has had the effect of making some of our predictions—for instance, our conviction that Wall Street's heyday was destined to fade—come to pass sooner rather than later. The implications we trace, including our projections of which occupations will move to the fore in coming years as investment banking and the legal profession dim, remain right on track.

In sum, we think our book is more relevant than ever. But don't take our word for it. Read it and, we hope, benefit from it. These are truly perilous times for investors, and the more you understand the underlying nature of the threats we face, the more likely that you will be among the relatively few who can survive in good shape.

Introduction

We want to start out by simply listing three facts that, taken as a whole, should scare all of us silly—or, more positively, prod us to action.

Fact 1: Globally, capitalism is out of the bag. Growing numbers of the world's 6.6 billion people are now actively seeking to equal Americans' high-consumption lifestyle that defines success in terms of how much one can afford to buy.

Fact 2: On average in China and India there are 25 vehicles per 1,000 inhabitants. This compares with around 140 per 1,000 in Brazil and with more than 800 per 1,000 in the United States.

Fact 3: Iran, another developing country that operates under a version of capitalism, is currently experiencing economic growth of 6 percent a year. At that rate, by 2013 this oil-exporting nation will become a net *importer* of oil.

Think through the implications of these three realities and you'll start to understand why the world is headed for a train wreck centered on pending massive shortages of commodities—and why it's so urgent to act now before it truly is too late.

* * *

The United States has long been living under *seven comforting but false assumptions* that are about to be exploded. In fact, the alarm clocks already have started to sound.

These assumptions are:
1. The world contains virtually limitless oil and mineral deposits. If supplies get too tight, we can always find more.
2. Governments and central banks know how to keep inflation under control.
3. Economic growth, perhaps with some occasional small interruptions, is on a perpetual upward track that will bring ever greater prosperity to all the world's inhabitants.
4. America's wealth is based on enduring advantages—including free enterprise and Yankee ingenuity—that will ensure we will always have the top spot in the global pecking order.
5. The national debt is no problem because economic growth will be so strong that we can pay it off…someday.
6. Technology can solve all our long-term problems. It's just a matter of putting more money into research.
7. Meanwhile, we can easily cope with any short-term emergencies. If we need new infrastructure, we'll build it. When it becomes urgent to switch to alternative energies, we'll turn our attention to it and get the job done. Ditto for reversing the trade deficit, funding government entitlement programs, or anything else. Therefore, too much planning ahead isn't necessary.

Unfortunately, all of these assumptions are about to be exposed as false. Within a decade, our worldview will be shattered. World economic growth will grind to a halt even as inflation soars to 25 percent or higher. The United States will revert from a postindustrial society to an industrial society and we will suffer wrenching changes to our way of life. And that's on a best-case basis—if we start to confront serious problems of worsening shortages in energy and other natural resources without further delay.

On a worst-case basis, there is no certainty that our civilization will survive. If we make the wrong choices now, we could be headed for the end of the line, like those old-fashioned pinball machines that, when you came to the end of your turn, imperiously flashed: GAME OVER. But with the pinball machines, you could always insert another coin and start again. We won't have that option.

Are we being too fatalistic? After all, people have been predicting the end of the world forever. This has given doomsday prophets, in some circles, a bad name.

However, we don't consider ourselves doomsdayers, and we're not predicting the inevitable end of the world—in fact, just the opposite: we're trying to sound an alarm so as to help avert things lurching hopelessly out of control. It's just that we look at today's world—and in particular at the rising prices and growing shortages not just of oil, the most glaring example for most people, but of virtually every other commodity as well—and believe that the problems we face are immensely more complex and difficult to solve than almost anyone seems to get. And they carry with them enormous implications for every aspect of our future, from international relations to financial markets.

We also believe that time is running out. The window of opportunity for solving problems of resource shortages is quite brief. The longer we wait, the more commodity prices will rise and the harder it will become to put into effect any solution. Why? Because any solution, no matter how technologically advanced, will inevitably require large inputs of the very resources that are becoming ever more difficult to find and afford.

Soothed by complacency and deep in denial, we've already waited far too long. Unable to imagine our vulnerability, we have come to depend on developing, politically immature countries for the oil and other resources that are our economic lifeblood. Now we are at their mercy even though in many cases they are our political enemies. It's an untenable position, and it will become ever harder to maintain it.

It's as simple as this: the longer we delay, the greater the pain and the lower the odds that we will be successful. We could have acted in the wake of previous oil crises, but we didn't. Now it's too late to make a painless transition to a post-oil world. Even if we begin now, we cannot avoid a tough transitional period that will involve economic turmoil—including, almost certainly, raging inflation, major lifestyle adjustments, and societal changes that are likely to be permanent.

But if we procrastinate much longer, the hardship will be even worse.

In 2008, with oil surging close to $150 a barrel and gasoline at the pump topping $4 a gallon, energy became a hot topic, as it has from time to time in the past. America's complacency was pricked just a bit. Or perhaps it would be more accurate to say that while we're still far more complacent than we should be, we're also experiencing a widespread growing sense of unease, a feeling that the future might be less certain than we like to believe. Sadly, however, the solutions being offered range from the myopic to the cynical to the simplistic.

For starters, inside government and out, there are those who argue that all we need to do is drill more and all will be fine. *Wrong.* On the other side of the political divide, there are those urging a windfall profits tax on oil companies—again, *wrong*. And there are those who support a gasoline tax holiday or who suggest that speculators in oil are the major culprits and that if we curb their role, oil prices will fall and stay low. *Wrong, wrong, wrong*.

Then there are those Wall Streeters—and I encounter them on a regular basis on television business news shows—who argue that the invisible and benign hand of capitalism will solve the problem. As oil prices rise, the profit motive will impel companies to move into alternative energies, and presto, we'll be back in business. I don't think there's a chance in the world they'll be proved right. It's simply too late in the day.

And finally, there are very bright and well-meaning commentators, including *New York Times* columnist Thomas L. Friedman and others, who urge an all-out Manhattan Project–like effort to develop and use on a wide scale the best alternative energies, and who applaud some recent moves by private entrepreneurs, such as oilman T. Boone Pickens's new commitment to natural gas–powered cars and wind energy. These writers are on the right track, or at least on the right side. But they miss a crucial point. *Our challenge has grown beyond the need to switch to alternative energies.* In fact, if we had the luxury—as would have been the case a few decades ago—of focusing narrowly on the one issue of energy, we'd actually be in great shape. Instead, we are now facing growing shortages of all commodities, not just oil. And this makes implementing a large-scale shift to alternative energies, though essential, enormously more difficult than almost anyone seems to realize.

The problems we face are urgent and complex. Oil shortages are inextricably tangled up with shortages and rising prices of other commodities, from iron ore to the more obscure metal tellurium—a critical ingredient in solar cells—to something as basic as freshwater, which is essential in virtually all mining processes and in the construction and running of nearly any kind of alternative energy you can think of.

It's this *combination* of resource shortages, impacting upon one another in a series of vicious circles, that could bring our civilization down. With resources becoming increasingly strained, we can't just plunge into any form of alternative energy, however appealing or green it might seem, without considering what resources it requires and where else those resources might be urgently needed. We need to understand the trade-offs and take into account the big picture. Otherwise, we could easily end up squandering our limited stores of resources on forms of alternative energy that can't be sustained over the longer term because some other resource essential to that energy isn't going to be available.

Wind energy, for instance, has obvious appeal as an affordable nonpolluting energy based on an endlessly renewable source. It seems to have great potential for helping to solve our energy needs and weaning us from our dependence on oil. But there are things to consider before assuming that we could always build the requisite network of wind turbines and all will be well.

One major stumbling block, for instance, is that wind turbines require a lot of steel, which is made from iron ore. And iron ore prices, driven by shortages and rising world demand, have soared even more than oil prices. Using wind energy on a small scale wouldn't stress iron ore supplies all that much—but it also wouldn't make much of a dent in our dependence on oil. On the other hand, if we were to try to implement wind energy on a large enough scale to make a real difference, rising iron ore prices would push the cost of wind-generated energy to unacceptable heights. In fact, it could become difficult even to find enough iron ore to build all the turbines needed. It would be foolish and shortsighted, therefore, to launch a major effort to switch to wind energy without assessing iron ore reserves and considering whether all the steel required could be put to more effective use elsewhere. And that's just one of the resources and trade-offs we'd have to consider. The same kind of analysis needs to be applied to other alternative energies as well.

The following example shows what we're facing. Suppose you lived at the bottom of a cliff, and day after day the only way to get food and water was to pull yourself twenty stories up on a rope, painstakingly gather a bit of food, and take it back down with you to safety. Now suppose that to do this you had to expend 2,500 calories, while the food you were able to procure on any one trip contained only 2,000 calories. Clearly, you'd be using up more energy than you'd be getting, and eventually you'd waste away to nothing.

The world could get to that point in terms of energy and other commodities—states that we call *Absolute Peak Oil* and *Absolute Peak Commodities*, because from then on, all production would cease. *Looking first at oil, here's why: it takes energy to get energy.* At a certain point, as oil gets harder to find and more difficult to extract, requiring a greater input of equipment and other materials that in themselves require energy to build and operate, getting a barrel of oil out of the ground will use up more than a barrel's worth of energy. A similar dynamic applies to other commodities as well. If we don't do something to avert Absolute Peak Oil and Absolute Peak Commodities in time, it will be Game Over for human civilization. We'll be effectively helpless.

What should we do, what can we do, and what is the world going to look like? First, we need to make a massive national, and per-haps international, commitment to determine which alternative energies have the most long-term potential—taking into account diminishing stores of other commodities—and then proceed with building them and the infrastructure they require. We have to act as if oil is running out tomorrow.

Second, we need to do everything we can to buy time for this effort, and to use the time wisely. We cannot afford to fall back into complacency and denial. Energy conservation can buy us some time, though not necessarily as much as many people think. Conservation tends to tamp down price increases and would encourage greater consumption in the developing world. We also could try to buy time by shedding some of the burdensome legal and regulatory complexities that add greatly to the cost of exploration and development. Most interesting of all, we could use the advanced applied mathematics now being developed by a few top thinkers to extract resources far more efficiently, that is, using up fewer resources in the process, than is now possible.

As for what the world will look like, we think that initially, as the developing world continues to push for rapid growth, we're in for a highly tumultuous period featuring steep inflation, which could, as we said earlier, reach 25 percent or more a year. Periodically, though, the inflationary uptrend could be interrupted by, or go hand in hand with, bouts of recession.

Eventually, global growth will hit a wall of resource shortages and will start to peter out for real. As a result, much of the world will never reach levels of consumption and production that the developed world now enjoys.

At some point in this process, as it becomes clear that resources are running ever lower, we will likely resort to rationing oil and other key commodities, possibly by international agreement, as the remaining supplies will need to be reserved for the most important uses.

Even if we manage to switch to alternative energies in

time—before Game Over—civilization still is unlikely ever to return to the same high level of material well-being that exists today in much of the developed world. Diminishing supplies of commodities other than energy will impose a permanent cap on consumption. For instance, even if we can harness the bountiful energy of the sun, we will have only a fixed supply of the metals and minerals needed to make solar devices as well as all the products we might wish to churn out. We'll have to budget our resources very carefully.

To put it differently, we think that society will be forced to become somewhat less complex than it is today, because simpler societies require less energy and fewer resources to support them. This won't necessarily be a bad thing. As complexity gets scaled back, it may mean fewer lawyers and MBAs and a greater call for people skilled in maintaining water supplies. Our culture may abandon the endless quest for "more" and find satisfaction with less.

If the world evolves in the way outlined above, we should be able to adapt and thrive. And if as you read you're wondering how this relates to you personally and how you can ensure your own personal survival, this book will present clear ways to protect yourself and your family financially even in the face of a jagged economic trajectory marked by super-high inflation. *Buying gold is our absolute top recommendation because it protects you during both inflation and deflation.* But there will be other profitable investments as well; we look at them in part 4.

The real catastrophe would be if we let things slide further without acting. If we arrive at Game Over before putting an entrenched network of alternative energies in place, our options will be few indeed. In that case we would expect a much more feral, embattled world, marked by wars over resources. It really could be the end of civilization.

Some of what's mentioned, of course, is speculation. But we think it's a lot less far-fetched than it might sound at first blush. What's not speculation are the looming resource shortages and the interdependencies among energy and other commodities. Let us show you the evidence so that you can draw your own conclusions. We urge you to protect yourself via the investments we recommend. And then, we hope you'll add your voice to those pleading that we tackle the problems of resource shortages before it's too late—before it's Game Over.

PART I

RESOURCE SHORTAGES:

Facing Facts

CHAPTER 1

Oil: Racing to Run-Out

We are headed toward a potentially catastrophic collision between hard reality and a worldview that has long refused to acknowledge it. Even on a best-case basis, this collision will involve a tumultuous, painful, and lengthy period of transition, marked by a decline in living standards and an increasingly out-of-control economy that careens from recession to periods of growth during which inflation reaches ever more stratospheric levels.

With luck, and if we face the situation sooner rather than later, we may emerge at the other end in reasonably decent shape, enjoying a likely simpler but sustainable economy based on renewable energies. Meanwhile, individuals who play their cards right during the coming turbulent years—putting their faith and money in the small handful of investments that will thrive as most others are plummeting in value—could become a new generation of wealthy Americans.

If we blow it, though, it could mean nothing less than the collapse of our civilization. It even could mean total annihilation in the wake of international turmoil and wars over ever-diminishing natural resources.

Yes, Peak Oil Is Real

It all starts with oil, and the first hard fact we need to face is that increasingly we don't have enough of it to meet the voracious demands of global growth. Oil has been essential to our economy for more than a century, and it's the lifeblood of the world's entire transportation network, powering hundreds of millions of cars and trucks as well as ships, tankers, airplanes, and trains. But in this decade, oil production has begun falling behind rising demand, which has caused the steep increases we've seen in oil prices. For many reasons, oil will never again be as plentiful and cheap as it used to be.

Many people on Wall Street and elsewhere still resist the whole notion of Peak Oil, which was first propounded in the 1950s by a geologist named M. King Hubbert. As Hubbert formulated it, oil production in a given field peaks when more than half the oil has been taken out. At that point, he argued, while you still can get more oil out of the field, annual production steadily and permanently declines.

The concept also can be more broadly applied to the world as a whole. Technically, this would lead to defining Peak Oil as the moment when global oil production reaches its maximum level. After that, production may stay flat for a time, or it may begin to fall. Either way, if demand rises, the result will be shortfalls that push oil prices continually higher. However, we prefer to define Peak Oil a bit differently: as the point at which increases in oil supply can no longer satisfy increases in demand. This definition, though slightly more amorphous than the technical definition, is more useful and relevant because it takes into account both the supply and demand of oil.

The usual response of those who reject the relevance of Peak Oil is to argue that technology will rescue us. Either it will let us get more oil more easily out of existing fields or it will help us find enough new fields to develop. But the evidence doesn't support this. In the United States, the most technologically advanced country in the world, production has been declining since the 1970s. If technology really could solve problems of oil shortages, we'd have cracked that nut by now. And we haven't.

Admittedly, you might argue that the real reason we haven't raised production has been limits imposed on drilling. There's no doubt that opening up areas now off-limits, such as the Arctic National Wildlife Refuge (ANWR), would add to production. But the process would be slow and in the end would add relatively little oil to the world. Opening up ANWR, for example, would take five to ten years to complete and would probably add no more than a million barrels a day to the world's oil production. At best this would satisfy just a small portion of additional demand, even assuming the world is growing fairly slowly. Moreover, given the time frame of five to ten years, this portion is likely to be considerably less than the drop in overall oil production that would be occurring. Meanwhile, the offshore areas that have become political bones of contention would take even longer to complete, would be very expensive to develop, and would offer only uncertain results. Even on a best-case basis, they, too, would do little to satisfy incremental demand.

Alarmingly, the evidence suggests that no matter how you define Peak Oil, the world today is fast reaching—and may already have reached—it. Even worse, a series of other factors are converging that could result not just in declining oil production but in an absolute halt. If we allow ourselves to reach this sorry stage, we will truly be at Game Over.

Earth's Gas Tank Is Half Empty

According to the best estimates, when our ancestors were just beginning to walk upright, the planet's crust held about 2.2 trillion barrels of oil. We have used up half of it in the past century alone.

Naturally, we went for the good stuff first: the light, sweet oil that was easy to get at and cheap to extract. But most of that is gone. From now on the quality goes down. Increasingly we've been relying on heavy, high-sulfur oil that costs more to refine, as well as on unconventional sources, such as tar sands, that take more money and resources to extract.

We have combed the earth so thoroughly that we are running out of places to drill for oil on land. Most of the undiscovered, close-to-shore oil already has been factored into the 2.2-trillion-barrel estimate. Now the search has headed out into the deepest oceans, where the costs go up considerably.

Two of the most recent, headline-grabbing oil finds are located in such places. The Jack 2 field in the Gulf of Mexico lies 20,000 feet below the ocean floor, which itself is 7,000 feet below sea level. *It would take over five miles of pipe to reach this oil*, and a rather expensive operation to pump it out.

Similarly, the Carioca field off the coast of Brazil, while potentially the third largest ever found, is also located under 7,000 feet of water and is more than 22,000 feet below the seabed. Building wells under these conditions presents enormous engineering challenges, and extraction costs will likely range from exorbitant to prohibitive.

And even then, the amount of oil in these two fields equals only what the world consumes every eighteen months.

As William J. Cummings of ExxonMobil put it, "All the easy oil and gas in the world has pretty much been found. Now comes the harder work in finding and producing oil from more challenging environments and work areas."

Scientists Weigh In

In claiming that the world is running out of affordable oil, we are in very good company. Most scientists express similar views (even if most stockbrokers don't).

For example, in the August 2003 issue of *New Scientist*, the Hydrocarbon Depletion Study Group from Sweden's Uppsala University reported the startling conclusion that actual world oil reserves are as much as 80 percent lower than is commonly thought.

The study, titled *Too Little Oil for Global Warming*, argues that there's so little oil left that burning all of it wouldn't produce enough carbon dioxide to alter the climate, much less melt polar ice caps. (Don't think this is good news for the environment, however. The study also points out that if we're forced to switch from oil and gas to coal, the resulting emissions *would* heat the atmosphere and lead to even worse air pollution.)

The Uppsala team aren't mavericks. In fact, they lead an ever-growing chorus of scientists bewailing the rapid disappearance of affordable oil. (By and large, the only scientists expressing an opposite view are those employed by oil industry firms, who may have an incentive to ignore impending shortages.) A typical sharp-tongued comment came from David Goodstein, vice provost of Cal Tech and author of *Out of Gas: The End of the Age of Oil* (voted one of the most notable books of the year by the *New York Times Book Review* in 2004). When asked whether huge new fields capable of meeting the world's future need for oil are waiting to be discovered, he replied, "Better to believe in the tooth fairy."

To be fair, we will continue to find new giant oil fields. (By giant we mean fields containing more than 500 million barrels of oil or 3 trillion cubic feet of natural gas.) But the rate of discovery has been dropping since 1965. And while it has picked up a little since the turn of the millennium, the latest projections suggest we will find fewer than half as many giant fields this decade as we did in the 1970s.

Most of the fields we are finding are extensions of existing fields or, as we pointed out earlier, deepwater, remote, or otherwise expensive to develop (Paul Mann, "Tectonic Setting of 79 Giant Oil and Gas Fields Discovered from 2000–2007: Implications for Future Discovery Trends," presentation of American Association of Petroleum Geologists, 2007). Meanwhile, production at older fields is winding down. U.S. oil production has been falling since the 1970s. North Sea oil production, which saved the world's bacon in the 1980s, is also declining, as is oil production throughout the non-OPEC (Organization of Petroleum Exporting Countries) world.

At the same time as supplies are becoming constrained, worldwide oil consumption continues to grow. *Since 2002, humanity has been consuming four times as much oil as we've been able to add to reserves.* This mismatch between demand and reserves is the major reason that over the past half decade or longer, oil production has started lagging demand. As a result, the excess oil supply, which was above 5 percent in 2002, is now close to zero. And within twenty years, according to most experts, demand will rise by over 50 percent.

We are clearly racing toward run-out. But, dishearteningly, hardly anyone in government or within the oil industry seems willing to raise the alarm in a loud enough voice to hit home.

How Close Are We?

Estimates of when the world will hit Peak Oil vary widely, from those who think that new discoveries and technology will give us to at least 2040—we think they're wildly off—to more pessimistic types who believe it already has happened. We think we very likely are already there, or if not that we'll be there very soon. That's because, for starters, with the possible exception of Canada and its tar sands, there is little chance that any Western country can significantly increase its oil production. And the tar sands, as we'll discuss in chapter 8, have many inherent limitations that make it unlikely that they will be able to take over oil's role in the world.

But what about oil from the Middle East? The International Energy Agency and the U.S. Department of Energy believe the world's demand for oil over the next decade or so will be met through higher oil production from that part of the world, and specifically from Saudi Arabia. The evidence is strong, though, that they are being way too optimistic.

First, if Saudi Arabia really does have spare capacity, it's odd that it hasn't increased oil output over the past several years. In late 2004, Saudi production reached nearly 9.8 million barrels a day. At that time oil was trading at under $60 a barrel. Since then, less than four years later, oil prices have nearly doubled. Yet the Saudis have *reduced* their daily output by nearly 600,000 barrels.

Such a decline, if deliberate, surely would have outraged oil importers, including the United States and China. Given that the Saudis depend so heavily on the U.S. for their defense, we can assume the U.S. has considerable influence with Saudi leaders. We think that if they could have produced more oil, they would have.

More clues that all is not right in the desert have come from recent statements from Sheikh Al-Naimi, Saudi Arabia's oil minister. In early 2008 he said the Saudis had put on hold any plans to raise oil production past 12.5 million barrels a day. Previously, though, the Saudis had said they would have no trouble raising production levels to 15 million barrels a day or even higher.

Saudi Arabia: Oil Production vs. Number of Rigs

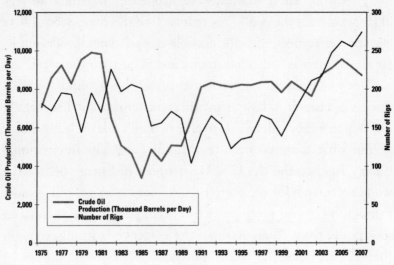

Sources: Bloomberg, Department of Energy

The above chart compares Saudi oil production with the number of oil rigs working in that country. As you can see, even though the number of rigs has risen dramatically in recent years, oil production has stagnated. To us, this disconnect implies that the Saudis have run out of additional capacity.

Matthew Simmons, energy banker and author of *Twilight in the Desert*, believes that many OPEC nations have been overstating their oil reserves for over a decade so that, under OPEC's quota rules, they would be allowed to produce more. Based on extensive research, including access to Saudi documents, Simmons argues that the Ghawar oil field, which accounts for about 70 percent of Saudi production, is in trouble and possibly on the verge of a dramatic decline.

Keep in mind that the Saudis aren't known for underestimating their ability to produce oil. Indeed, it's in their interest to overstate their abilities, as it keeps their position in the world secure.

United States: Oil Production vs. Number of Rigs

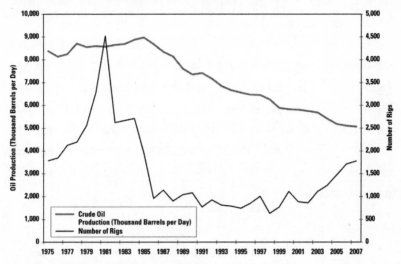

Sources: Bloomberg, Department of Energy

And if Saudi production has in fact peaked, there is virtually no chance that global oil production can keep pace with demand, meaning we are already at Peak Oil. Among other things, this means that the price of energy and everything else will accelerate more rapidly.

Those who claim the Saudis are better positioned than we think don't offer much of a case. An executive at the major Italian oil company Eni, for instance, made the claim in *Foreign Affairs* that there must be plenty of oil left in Saudi Arabia because wildcatting—drilling experimental wells in areas not known to be productive—had just begun there. But the history of oil production in the United States suggests this argument doesn't hold water: oil wildcatting and a commensurate increase in rigs didn't occur in the U.S. until after 1970, when production had already passed its peak.

Even the most strenuous doubters of anything smacking of

Peak Oil, such as money management firm and broker Sanford Bernstein, lend support, despite themselves, to the notion that the Ghawar field could be losing ground. Bernstein recently commissioned an aerial survey of the Ghawar field and, based on the photographs, concluded that Saudi production declines were not "significant." The reality, though, is that *any* decline is significant. Once a field starts to decline, the rate at which production falls can accelerate sharply at any time. If production at Ghawar, the most important oil field in the world, has begun falling, the clear conclusion is that the Saudis will be unable to meet increased future demand.

Absolute Peaks

Peak Oil certainly isn't a desirable state, but it's nonetheless one we can live with. With Peak Oil, we're talking about a situation where it still makes economic sense to pump oil even though rising demand and lagging production keep pushing oil prices higher. Theoretically, as oil supplies fall behind demand, there is no limit to how high energy prices could reach (though there is a limit to how much the average person can afford to pay for the necessities of life).

But unless we take effective action very soon, rising oil prices ultimately will be superseded by something much worse: *Absolute Peak Oil*. Once we hit Absolute Peak Oil, it will make no sense at all to keep drilling for oil, because we'd be forced to expend more energy than we could obtain from our efforts. *At a certain point, to get a barrel out of the ground, we'd have to invest more than a barrel's worth of energy to pump, refine, and truck it to the local gas station.* Oil will exist, but it will be tantalizingly out of reach for all practical purposes.

How much time might we have before hitting Absolute

Peak Oil? If we don't develop alternative energies fairly rapidly—managing to avert the worst-case scenarios brought on by the vicious circles of multiple resource shortages that we describe in the next chapter—it could be fairly soon. One point of reference: if we keep using up oil at the current rate of around 31 billion barrels a year, by 2040 there will be no oil left in the ground at all. That's the outer limit of time we might have left.

Absolute Peak Oil would be a dire situation. It isn't going to happen overnight, though, and it will be preceded by some striking changes in how the world goes about its business. Among these changes, we expect that at some point prior to reaching Absolute Peak Oil, whatever oil is still available no longer will go to just anyone willing to pay for it. It probably wouldn't be sold, for instance, to owners of private automobiles and trucks. Instead, we envision the possibility of governments getting together to reserve the oil for the most essential uses. Unthinkable? Don't bet against it.

That's why it's critical that between now and then we put into place new sources of energy for our cars, trucks, factories, homes, and everything else. If we don't, our economy, and indeed our civilization, will grind to a halt. It will be Game Over, and not just for the American dream, but for the dreams of the entire world.

Unfortunately, though, as we'll show, the very same things that make it essential that we develop alternative energy on a huge scale are also making this feat increasingly difficult to accomplish. We have at best a fairly small window of opportunity—the time between now and Absolute Peak Oil and Absolute Peak Commodities. If we don't take advantage of that sliver of time, it will be too late. Why is this window of time so critical? Because it will be the last chance we have to extract more resources from the earth than those we use up during the process of extraction.

Meanwhile, as prices of energy and other commodities continue to rise, we face a likely jagged trajectory of economic extremes that will be very hard—though not impossible—for individuals to come through intact. As we said earlier, expect stretches of growth where inflation reaches greater and greater heights interrupted by periods of recession. Not a great outlook. But if we don't tackle resource shortages soon and in a serious concerted way, it will only get worse.

CHAPTER 2

Vicious Circles: Oil, Metals, and Minerals

Oil isn't the only critical commodity that is becoming both scarcer and more expensive. The same applies to a whole range of metals and minerals that are essential to our civilization and the technologies on which it depends. The table on page 26 presents sixteen of them, indicating how many years' worth of supplies is likely left for each.

At present rates of consumption, we will run out of antimony, indium, lead, silver, tantalum, tin, and uranium in the next four to twenty years. Within forty years we'll be out of chromium, copper, and zinc. Nickel and platinum will soon follow. For the sixteen metals and minerals as a whole, on average we have roughly twenty-five years of supply left. And that doesn't take into account the likely increases in consumption that will occur over that time.

As with oil, the run-out won't be total. The world will never completely be out of any particular mineral. Metals (other than alloys) are elements that cannot be destroyed: only chemically bonded in different ways. Even if all underground deposits were exhausted, there still would be traces of copper, iron, and even

Industrial Commodities: Past, Present, Future

Commodity	% U.S. Imported 1999	2006	% Production or Reserves in Developing Countries	Years of Reserves if World Consumes at Half the U.S. Rate
Aluminum	30	44	82.0	n/a
Antimony	85	100	97.5	13
Chromium	75	75	99.9	40
Copper	27	50	86.0	38
Gallium	100	99	90.0	n/a
Germanium	45	80	95.0	n/a
Indium	100	100	57.0	4
Lead	20	50	52.0	8
Nickel	60	60	70.0	57
Platinum	92	95	97.5	42
Rhodium	92	95	97.5	n/a
Silver	14	65	80.0	9
Tantalum	100	100	45.0	20
Tin	85	80	96.0	17
Uranium	76	84	75.0	19
Zinc	30	65	56.0	34
Average	64.4	77.6	79.8	25.1

Sources: The Complete Investor *(Stephen Leeb, editor),* U.S. Geological Survey, New Scientist

platinum in the dust that covers every street, buried in landfills, or dissolved in the oceans. However, no operation could possibly produce enough metals from such sources to supply our expanding world. It would simply take too much energy to be worthwhile.

Before their reserves run low, the countries with the highest endowments of critical minerals are due for their day in the sun. Until their stores get depleted, they will command any price the market will bear. This, in conjunction with soaring energy prices, will spearhead the super-high inflation that we believe lies ahead and that we discuss in detail in part 3.

But try to talk about the steep shortfalls in metals and minerals that lie just over the horizon and, as with energy, you run head-on into complacency. The usual response from Wall Streeters and others, if these facts are brought up, is to blithely say that as prices rise, we'll simply increase exploration and find more of these resources. And certainly this is true—up to a point. Rising commodity prices will encourage the development of additional reserves, making it profitable to undertake mining operations in deposits that at lower prices weren't economically attractive.

There's a catch, though, and it's a huge one. *These metals and minerals are mutually interdependent with one another and, even more significantly, with energy.* If it were just a matter of one or two commodities becoming scarce, the situation wouldn't be so dire. The problem is that the intricate interdependencies that exist will create a vicious circle that will send the prices of all commodities simultaneously to the moon, making it immensely more difficult and perhaps impossible to develop enough new reserves to sustain civilization at levels we assume to be our birthright.

An Island Fable

To understand how this vicious circle will unfold, let's use a simple illustration. Imagine a small island blessed with three primary resources: freshwater from annual rainfall, abundant energy from tar sand deposits, and mines replete with metals and minerals. With these resources, the inhabitants have no problem growing enough food and providing themselves with shelter and other comforts.

Eventually, though, the population grows to where all the freshwater is being used for drinking and irrigation, with nothing left over. Soon, the islanders realize, they might not have enough for their needs. But they think they have the answer: using the energy from tar sands, they can extract metals from their mines and build desalination plants to convert some seawater into freshwater.

It's a little tricky, though, because producing each resource—metals, tar sands, and water—depends on each of the other two. Water and metals are needed to extract oil from tar sands; water and oil are needed to obtain and refine the metals; and energy and metals are needed to build and run the desalination plants. But the islanders calculate that they have enough resources to build the new plant. Once it is operational, they can increase their metal and oil production and still end up with enough additional water to meet the needs of their growing population. They build the desalination plant and for a while all goes well.

But nothing lasts forever. Over time, the tar sands become somewhat depleted. The islanders are forced to move to the lower-grade deposits, which require significantly greater inputs of water and metals to yield oil. Producing the extra steel needed for that energy-dredging effort requires, in turn, more energy and water. With more and more water now needed to produce both oil and steel, the island needs bigger desalinators—but these, in turn, will take more energy and minerals.

In yet another blow, the best mines start to become exhausted, meaning the islanders have to devote extra oil and metals to explore for new mineral deposits and build new mines. These new mines, though, are lower grade—not surprising, since naturally the islanders mined the best deposits first—meaning they require more energy to work. Meanwhile, the population continues to grow, further increasing the demand for water and other resources.

At a certain point, the islanders realize they're stuck in a vicious circle. Trying to get enough of any one resource overtaxes supplies of the other two. The more they try, the tighter the noose gets. The only way out would be if they had a limitless supply of energy, enabling them to obtain enough minerals—through exploration, recycling, even extracting them from seawater—and to desalinate enough water. But the tar sands aren't limitless and they are fast running low.

The final upshot: eventually the resources needed to produce metal, water, or oil exceed the value of the resources produced—in other words, the islanders, to get anything out, need to put more than that amount in, an obviously losing proposition. And at that point, it's over. Production of all three resources hits a permanent peak, and the islanders suffer serious shortages of everything.

Or to put it in our terminology, they have moved from Peak Energy and Peak Commodities to that grim state of Absolute Peak Energy and Absolute Peak Commodities: Game Over.

Warning Signs

This fable is a streamlined version of what is actually happening today on island Earth. As some commodities have become scarcer and thus more expensive, it is making it more expensive to find, develop, and produce other commodities, causing their production to slow. Soon most critical commodities will become increasingly scarce. In conjunction with rising energy costs, the resulting cascade of higher mineral costs threatens to eventually make all exploration and production too expensive to continue.

We've had clear warning signs already. In the first quarter of 2008, for instance, the leading aluminum producer, Alcoa, reported record revenues, not surprising given that aluminum prices have tripled since the start of the decade. But earnings were very disappointing as higher energy prices added substantially to costs.

What applies to Alcoa applies to other aluminum companies as well. In producing aluminum, energy is the single biggest expense. To process one ton of aluminum requires around 35 barrels of oil or its energy equivalent. True, recycling aluminum requires just 6.5 percent of the energy needed for primary processing. But recycling supplies only about 40 percent of the world's aluminum supply.

Aluminum is the second-most-used metal in construction, and demand for it is increasing rapidly. By the end of this decade the world will be using about 40 million tons of the metal. Processing it will require the equivalent of 875 million barrels of oil a year, or more than 2 percent of oil production. It seems clear that aluminum prices are headed far higher still.

Higher energy prices are adding to the cost of producing other commodities as well, negatively impacting the earnings of producers. Cost overruns from higher prices have caused new mines, such as NovaGold's Galore Creek project in Canada and Petaquilla's copper project in Panama, to be put on hold despite record prices for gold and copper.

For producers to develop new supplies, commodity prices must be high enough to cover their costs and leave enough profit to attract investors. Otherwise, new supplies won't be developed. But as rising energy prices eat into profit margins, it becomes ever harder to develop new resources. And with no new resources to replace those that become exhausted, commodities will continue to grow scarcer and more expensive.

A Two-Way Street

The above examples show how rising energy prices have started to choke off some production of metals and minerals. But as in our island fable, this is a two-way street, and the reverse is true as well—rising prices of metals and minerals have begun to hit at energy production.

Just as on the island, developing energy resources requires big inputs of other commodities, including iron ore, zinc, copper, and even small amounts of some precious metals, including silver. As rising oil prices make these commodities more expensive, it also becomes more expensive to develop additional energy resources. A vicious circle indeed.

Here's an example. As reported in a *New York Times* article, in May 2004, Duke Energy began making plans to build two coal-fired plants in North Carolina. By November 2006, however, the company had canceled one of the plants. The reason it gave: construction costs had risen more than 80 percent as a result of higher prices for copper, nickel, stainless steel, and other commodities (Matthew L. Wald, "Costs Surge for Building Power Plants," July 10, 2007). Similarly, the costs of building other energy facilities, from nuclear plants to wind turbines, also have shot up in recent years.

Saudi oil minister Sheikh Al-Naimi has said that the cost of boosting oil production by just one additional barrel a day has climbed from about $2,000 earlier this decade to about $10,000. And we doubt this figure includes many of the costs associated with building the infrastructure needed to accommodate the labor force brought in to work on such projects, such as desalination plants to provide drinking water. If you factored in these necessary expenses, the total cost per additional barrel could be considerably higher. And for those of you not inclined to take the word of the Saudis on such matters, the rise in oil production costs has been confirmed by numerous other sources.

For instance, U.S. oil companies, too, have been reporting comparable increases in production costs. Exxon, for example, the world's largest publicly held oil company, announced that, in the first quarter of 2008, its net income had reached an all-time record of nearly $10.9 billion, a 17 percent jump from the previous year's results. While at first glance that might sound good, remember that over the same period oil prices rose more than 70 percent. One would have thought that the profits would have matched that rise in prices, but no. In other words, the company showed a surprising inability to profit from rising oil prices.

There are two main reasons why Exxon failed to generate higher earnings, and together they strongly suggest the rapid approach of both Peak Oil and Absolute Peak Oil. First, the company's costs rose as spending on exploration jumped 30 percent. And second—and despite this huge rise in spending on exploration—oil production actually fell by 5 percent, a massive one-year drop and a major drag on revenues.

How should we interpret the fact that the largest and arguably best-run oil company in the world is spending enormous and growing amounts of money to ward off a large decline in production? One conclusion is that the oil industry may be reaching the point where no amount of money can keep production from falling. If so, it implies that the portion of the world where the oil majors have access—that is, every oil field outside the control of state-run entities, such as those in the Middle East—may be at or near Peak Oil and possibly Absolute Peak Oil.

(Note that this alone is a strong reason why investors no longer should regard major integrated oil companies as growth investments. Their future profit growth will derive solely from rising oil prices. Yet with production declining, these profits will continue to be unable to keep pace with rising energy prices. We'll have more to say about this in part 4.)

Even if we're not at Peak Oil yet, the vicious circle encompassing energy and other commodities means we'll get there soon enough, as the cost of developing new oil supplies continues to rise. Again, some concrete examples show why this isn't just a theoretical concern. In the preceding chapter we mentioned the

Carioca oil deposit, discovered in 2007 off the coast of Brazil. Let's assume for a moment that oil prices need to be over $150 a barrel for this deposit to be profitable, after deducting the cost of the energy, labor, and materials needed to develop and operate it. Now let's suppose that oil prices do hit $150. Should the companies with the rights to this deposit start building wells?

Not necessarily. The $150 figure is only a static estimate based on today's prices. By the time actual drilling begins, the costs could have escalated sharply. In fact, they would likely escalate—and this is the crux of our argument—simply because the act of assembling the massive amount of labor and equipment to develop Carioca and similar fields around the world will add to the scarcity of the energy and other commodities needed as inputs.

It could well be that the vicious circle will make the cost of drilling profitably rise faster than the price of oil. When the amount of energy (including the energy that goes into the materials required for wells, pipes, and other materials) needed to produce energy is more than the amount of energy produced, you've reached Absolute Peak Oil—as well as Absolute Peak Commodities. And when this occurs, the global production of commodities that sustain civilization will start to come to a halt.

CHAPTER **3**

Water Is a Commodity, Too

R emember how, in our island fable, the islanders' problems began with water? As the island's population grew, the available freshwater became insufficient to meet all its needs. Once again, this foreshadows what is happening in the real world today.

Water is sometimes slighted as a resource, because it doesn't yet fetch high prices—in fact, in many places, it's still free. But in a number of obvious ways it's the most critical resource of all: without water, the human race and most other life as well would quickly cease to exist. Beyond directly nourishing human life, water has many other essential uses that keep it deeply entwined in the vicious circle involving energy and other commodities. Like them, supplies of water are starting to fall behind rapidly growing demand, making water yet another thorny issue that will tax our ability to find answers to the growing problem of resource shortages.

Contamination, Droughts, Floods

As you may recall from your fifth-grade science class, the Earth's surface is about 70 percent water. Sounds promising, right? The problem is that all but a tiny fraction of that water—around 3 percent—is salt water, which, unless treated, isn't much good to us. Moreover, even much of that 3 percent sliver isn't accessible because it's locked away in glaciers.

Before examining the issues that affect the remaining freshwater supply, it's worth looking at the natural process known as the water cycle. If we hopped aboard a water molecule, we would find ourselves carried around to lakes, streams, dirt, aquifers, etc. Eventually, we would move into the oceans, where after waiting a good long time we would evaporate—as freshwater—into the atmosphere. Soon we would fall back to earth—or reenter the ocean—as rain or snow, and the whole process would start again.

Nowhere in our journey was our molecule ever destroyed. Unlike fossil fuels, which are gone forever once we combust them for energy, the amount of freshwater on Earth is more or less constant. The water we drink, for example, doesn't just sit in our body forever. It is excreted and rejoins the water cycle. The same goes for the water used in agriculture and industry. It seldom if ever disappears.

That's the good news. The bad news, though, is that while freshwater can't be destroyed, much of it is—or can become—virtually useless to human beings unless we devote a lot of money, energy, and natural resources to making it work for us. For one thing, water can get contaminated. Throughout modern history, examples of large-scale water contamination abound. One such case was Europe's Rhine River in the 1970s. As cities dotting its banks dumped waste into the Rhine, its water became unusable. The situation got so bad, in fact, that an area of the river near Cologne, Germany, was declared a danger zone.

The other major problem is that much of the Earth's freshwater is inconveniently located. Water moves around with scant regard for where we most need it. While some areas are plagued by drought, others must contend with floods, an overabundance of water that does no one any good and is actually destructive. Moreover, recently there have been some unfortunate—and perhaps permanent—shifts in where water is located.

For instance, freshwater tables are falling in the three nations that produce most of the world's grain: the United States, China, and India. Many of the world's great rivers, including the Colorado, the Yellow, the Ganges, and the Indus, are emptied or reduced to a trickle before they reach the sea (Lester R. Brown, "Draining Our Future: The Growing Shortage of Freshwater," *The Futurist*, May 1, 2008). Though the water that used to be in these locations has found its way into some other part of the water cycle, that is no consolation to the people who locally depend on these water sources for irrigation and other uses or who eat the food grown in these regions. Other locations, of course, find themselves with far too much water, as did the midwestern U.S. during recent devastating floods.

Contamination, droughts, and floods aren't new. But with the emergence of the developing world, they are becoming more worrisome. As the developing world gains in both population and wealth, its demands on water are burgeoning—for drinking and sanitation, for food, and as an essential aid in the extraction of all the natural resources needed for economic growth. Add to this the fact that industrialization in the developing world is contaminating more of the world's water supplies, and it's easy to see why the planet is getting closer to the day when we might not have enough freshwater to go around.

Food and Industry

Let's talk about food in relation to water. As per capita incomes rise in developing countries, their growing middle classes want to eat better. In particular, they want to eat more meat. Unfortunately, producing meat requires a lot more water than the amounts needed to grow the agricultural products that traditionally have made up the bulk of the diet of poorer populations. That's because meat requires not only the water that livestock need to drink directly but also the water to grow the crops the animals eat. According to Rockefeller University demographer Joel Cohen's book *How Many People Can the Earth Support?*, on a per-calorie basis, meat is about ten times more water-intensive to produce than are agricultural products such as rice and grains.

The extra strains on freshwater supplies already are being felt, and it will get far worse. Worldwide water consumption has tripled in the last fifty years, with 70 percent of it used for irrigation (Brown, "Draining Our Future"). Currently, more than a billion people in developing nations lack access to safe drinking water, and more than 2 billion lack proper sanitation ("A Fresh Approach to Water," *Nature*, March 20, 2008).

Industrial demand for water has been rapidly expanding as well, further stressing supplies. Water is a vital requirement in just about any industry you can name, including energy. All standard generating plants, whether gas-, coal-, or nuclear-fueled, require tremendous amounts of water. In the United States, some 40 percent of our freshwater is used for cooling power plants—more than 500 billion liters a day (ibid.).

With the world's nascent economies consuming more and more energy, there is a rising call on water supplies for this purpose alone. And while getting conventional oil out of the ground requires a lot of water, the prognosis is likely to get even worse as we look about for other sources of energy to replace oil.

For instance, many believe that Canada's vast tar sands can rescue us as oil shortages worsen. The sands certainly contain considerable amounts of oil reserves. But developing and using tar sands requires enormous inputs of water, both to extract them from the earth and to burn them in power plants. Each barrel of oil extracted from tar sands uses 4.5 times the volume of water as a barrel of conventional oil (Jeffrey Simpson, "Alberta's Tar Sands Are Soaking Up Too Much Water," *The Globe and Mail*, July 5, 2006). Methods for extracting oil from shale also are water-intensive, using between 2.1 and 5.2 times the volume of water as the volume of the shale produced (James T. Bartis, et al., "Oil Shale Development in the United States: Prospects and Policy Issues," *Infrastructure, Safety and the Environment*, RAND Corporation, 2005: 72).

Moreover, industrial growth is a double whammy for water. Not only does industry have a voracious appetite for water, industrial use results in more water being contaminated. We mentioned the Rhine in the 1970s. In today's world, developing nations are seeing a lot of this type of severe water pollution. Take India, for example. Vadodara, the third-largest city in India and one that has experienced tremendous industrial expansion, has also seen severe pollution of the Vishwamitri River that runs through it, because the city's industries dump their waste there. And the town of Ichalkaranji has seen such industrial pollution of its Pachganga River that the Indian government has declared the water unsuitable for drinking.

China, too, has witnessed its fair share of water contamination from emerging industry. An explosion at a chemical plant in November 2005 leaked toxins into the Songhua River, ruining the drinking water of the 3.4 million people in the city of Harbin. In 2007, it was revealed that Lake Tai, one of the largest lakes in China, had become filled with pond scum and cyanobacteria, caused in large part by the local chemical plants in the area. More than 2 million people who depended on Lake Tai for their freshwater were affected by this calamity.

With more water needed than ever before in humanity's history, clearly it is becoming urgent that we find ways to obtain more usable supplies by overcoming problems of contamination and location. But while the technologies to fix these problems have been around for a long time, our ability to effectively employ them is severely hampered by the natural resources—including water—these technologies consume.

Squeezing Out More

In theory, solving the world's water problems boils down to purifying dirty water and moving water from water-rich regions to drought-prone regions. At first glance, this might not sound like such a problem. We have long had the technology to clean and transport water. Here's a quick summary of the major water technologies available.

There are two main water purification technologies in use today: *reverse osmosis* and *multistage flash distillation*. Distillation involves boiling water into steam and channeling it into a clean location where it condenses, leaving its impurities behind. In reverse osmosis plants, the dirty water is pushed through a membrane that filters out the impurities, much like a strainer.

Technology for transporting water has existed for millennia—think about the Roman aqueducts. Modern means are a bit more sophisticated, using pumps to push water through pipes. Barrels of water can also be moved around via land vehicles, and in fact, water can even be transported across continental divides; so-called water bags filled with freshwater have been dragged through the Mediterranean Sea from Turkey to Cyprus, for instance.

In addition to building more desalination plants and water transportation systems, water conservation efforts have also been proposed to prevent water from escaping from where it is needed. The Organisation for Economic Co-operation and Development (OECD) has authored two major reports that look at the world's need for freshwater. They recommend massive expenditures on water recycling, repairing leaky pipes, extending pipes, and maintaining aquifers. Altogether, these experts say, over the foreseeable future the world will need to spend more than half a trillion dollars a year on water infrastructure.

That's a lot of money. Beyond that, though, is the stumbling block that we invoked in our island fable. Repairing and creating the infrastructure to upgrade our water supplies will require huge inputs of metal and energy. But water, as we've seen, is needed for obtaining metals and energy, and thus the infrastructure intended to save water will in itself create new demands for water—once again, that old vicious circle.

Ditto for desalinating water: it takes a lot of energy. Dr. Allan R. Hoffman of the Department of Energy estimated in 2003 that about 40 percent of the cost of running reverse osmosis desalination plants—which is the most energy-efficient kind of desalination plant—comes from electricity. Furthermore, energy is also needed to transport water via pipes. It is not at all clear how the world will be able to harness all the energy needed to clean and transport water, especially because so many energy sources themselves require bucketloads of water.

On this last point, the recent article in *Nature* cited earlier notes:

> Already, freshwater concerns are starting to affect U.S. electric power generation. The current severe drought in the Southeast has threatened the cooling water supplies of more than 24 of the nation's 104 nuclear reactors. Not surprisingly, proposals to add additional thermoelectric

power plants in the region are meeting increased public resistance....A severe drought in France in 2003 caused the loss of up to 15 percent of nuclear power generating capacity for five weeks.... In the future, the energy sector will find itself increasingly in competition with other water users for limited freshwater resources.

Many forms of energy production also strain water supplies by causing pollution. One of the most notorious offenders is coal mining. Coal mining operations are known to unleash the sulfur compound pyrite into nearby rivers, doing tremendous damage to local water supplies. According to the United States Geological Survey, Pennsylvania's coal mines have contaminated over 2,400 miles of streams, as well as the state's groundwater reserves. And burning large amounts of any fossil fuel damages water supplies through acid rain. Directly or indirectly, conventional forms of energy production and use place great strains on the world's water resources.

As we struggle to produce more food and provide sufficient water to more households at the same time as we need to generate greater amounts of electricity, the strain on our water supplies will become increasingly evident. Already, there are portents. Atlanta, for instance, considered the capital of the southeastern United States, experienced an unprecedented drought in 2008. Many believe the city is on the verge of a catastrophic water shortage within the next several years.

Energy and water are mutually dependent resources, and it's this mutual dependency that makes tackling either problem so difficult. Further complicating matters is that metals are also a critical part of the mix. In particular, titanium is a vital component in water desalination systems. It also happens to be one of the most energy-intensive metals in the world; it takes a mind-boggling 150 barrels of oil to process a ton of the stuff. Furthermore, titanium mining has also been the cause of water pollution. In 2006, major titanium mining operations in Vietnam and China were shut down due to the environmental damage they had caused to local water supplies.

Much like the islanders in our story, civilization today is in a terrible jam. With all the additional demands for food and industry being brought to bear by the developing world, we need to increase our capacity to clean and move massive amounts of water, produce more energy, and mine more metals. But the vicious circle linking these resources means that trying to increase supplies of any one of them places even more demands on the other two. *Water, which is so often taken for granted, is a key resource that we can't ignore.* Increasingly, it will be a major constraint on efforts to solve problems of looming shortages in energy and other commodities.

There are no easy answers, and any solution will involve intricate trade-offs. Ultimately, the only way to slash through this complex Gordian knot will be through the development of renewable energies. But these, too, will depend on water. The longer we wait, the tougher the trade-offs will become, and if we wait until we've reached Absolute Peak Oil and Absolute Peak Commodities, no trade-offs in the world may be enough to save us.

In part 2 we look at a whole range of potential alternative energies and consider, among other things, how much water and input of other resources each one will require. First, though, let's look at why we're so certain that, for a good while longer, the demand for natural resources will continue to surge.

CHAPTER 4

The Developing World

Not all that long ago, it was easy to ignore China and India. After all, huge though they were in area and population, they were essentially nonplayers on the world's economic stage, irrelevant to our concerns.

That, obviously, has changed in a big way. Today China and India—which we've dubbed "Chindia"—together constitute a major world economic powerhouse, whose surging growth is at the heart of global economic trends. Demand from Chindia, along with that from other developing nations, largely accounts for the steep rises in the price of oil and other resources that we've seen for much of this decade, as Chindia's rapid growth feeds off huge inputs of energy and every resource imaginable. The near certainty that the developing world will keep pushing to consume more for as long as it can is a big part of why we're approaching Peak Oil and Peak Commodities as well as Absolute Peaks. And by extension, it's also a big part of why we'll be forced to operate in an environment of high and rising inflation for a good deal of the time ahead.

But the implications for the world's future economic outlook don't end there. Rapid growth in the developing world will continue for as long as it can, but that won't be forever. As the developing world scrabbles its way up the economic ladder, eating up more precious and finite resources in the process, it ultimately will hit a wall of resource limits. It will cease being able to keep growing as it had been doing because the resources needed to sustain growth will no longer be affordable or even available at any price. At that point global growth will start decelerating.

If before we reach that juncture we've made the momentous switch to alternative energies, the world might not end up in such a bad state, though it is likely to look considerably different from today. With sufficient, affordable, renewable energies in place, the world may settle down at a lower but sustainable level of consumption.

If, however, we've stubbornly and shortsightedly continued refusing to face the reality of shrinking energy supplies, the outlook will be infinitely bleaker. We'll be facing Absolute Peaks and a possible collapse of civilization as we know it, with living standards dropping precipitously and developed and developing nations alike possibly slipping into chaos.

We look at these potential economic scenarios, both the nearer-term and longer-term ones, in greater detail in part 3. Here, though, we want to zoom in on the developing world, looking at where it has been and where it is headed, and present some of the numbers involved. That's the only way to grasp the immensity of the developing world's significance, because, from whatever angle you examine growth in the developing world and its likely impact on energy and resource consumption going forward, the figures are staggering. They make it plain that the emergence of the developing world has been a real game changer—one with the potential to lead to Game Over for the world at large.

Avid for the Good Life

Recall that we opened this book by presenting three simple but telling facts. Two of the three bear directly on the demand side of the energy and commodities equation, explaining why the explosive demand for resources that we've seen already is only going to intensify.

The first fact was that capitalism is running rampant in the developing world, as its inhabitants increasingly define themselves in terms of how much they can afford to buy. The second fact was that China and India have 25 vehicles per 1,000 people, compared to 140 vehicles per 1,000 people in Brazil and more than 800 per 1,000 in the United States. And we could easily have pointed out any number of similar statistics as well. For instance: China has only one-third as many cell phones per capita as does the U.S. and only one-ninth as many computers per capita.

Now throw in one more reality, and the implications for the demand for resources are plain. China, whose growth has averaged a sensational 10 percent a year over the past several years, and India, growing at only a slightly lower 8 percent average rate, have a combined population of some 2.4 billion people. The developing world overall has a population of 5.4 billion people. This means that every tiny increase in the developing world's per capita consumption translates into truly mammoth numbers of additional products, whether these are cars, cell phones, computers, or anything else. All of these products eat up resources, both in making and in using them—pushing us ever closer to the point where serious scarcities could arise and overwhelm us.

There is every sign that per capita consumption in the developing world will keep rising. Increasingly, middle-class Chinese and Indian families—a stratum that is expanding rapidly—feel they should have a TV, a cell phone, a car, not to mention a refrigerator, an air conditioner, and more. To maintain political stability, governments in China and India must help their populations obtain these material goods by continuing to promote policies that encourage growth. China needs to keep economic growth above 7 percent a year or risk massive unemployment, a threat its government won't be willing to incur. In 2006, there were 94,000 major demonstrations in China (more than 50 people each), up 9 percent from the year before, indicating economic and social dissatisfaction. If these protests occurred under conditions of fast growth, it's clear that dissatisfaction would become an even greater threat if growth slowed. The Chinese are demanding jobs and a more prosperous lifestyle, and the government knows it must deliver to keep the peace.

Let's look at recent trends more closely, with the help of some tables, beginning with a look at how far Chindia has come already, which happens to be a lot further than most people realize.

The first table, Gross Domestic Product and Purchasing Price Power of China and India vs. the United States, looks at Chindia's Gross Domestic Product (GDP) compared to that of the United States. As you know, GDP represents the total value of all the goods and services a country produces each year, whether they have been consumed or invested to generate goods for future consumption. Until 2007, GDP in the U.S. surpassed that of any other individual country, whether you looked at it in terms of the actual numbers of goods produced or the dollar value of those goods.

In 2007, though, Chindia overtook the United States in terms of actual goods produced. This is a very big deal, but many economists and commentators have failed to appreciate its significance because they are accustomed to expressing GDP as a dollar figure. And in terms of dollars, Chindia's ascent hasn't been as rapid. Rather, it has crept up to where its GDP, which was just 12 percent of U.S. GDP in 1989, reached 17 percent of U.S. GDP in 2007. Not all that notable.

Gross Domestic Product and Purchasing Price Power of China and India vs. the United States

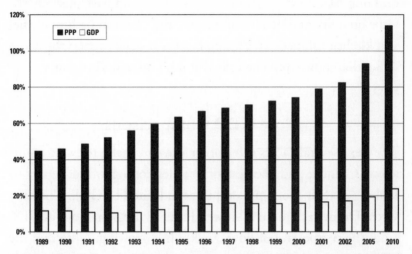

What It Means: In terms of actual goods produced (black bars), Chindia has just passed the United States. Most commentators do not realize this because they are accustomed to thinking only in terms of dollars (white bars).
Sources: World Bank, The Complete Investor *(Stephen Leeb, editor)*

However, over the same period, the true unit value of the goods produced in Chindia—the actual numbers of computers, TVs, and so forth—has rocketed from 43 percent to more than 100 percent—a very big deal indeed. It means that Chindia's call on resources for its manufacturing sector now surpasses that of the United States. The U.S., of course, remains a major world economic power. But it's not the only power, and it's less powerful than it used to be, in that, increasingly, what happens within the U.S. has less influence on global economic trends than was the case only a short while back.

In case you're wondering why there would be a difference between the two measures, units and dollar value, it's simple: because Chindia is essentially a less expensive part of the world than the United States, things there are valued more cheaply in dollar terms. By way of analogy, think of a house somewhere in the middle of, say, Arkansas, and then think of the exact same house plunked down in the tony and ultraexpensive resort town of Southampton on Long Island's south shore. The houses could have precisely the same quantity and quality of lumber, the identical bathroom tiles and kitchen cabinets, and so on, but it wouldn't matter: the house in Southampton would be valued at millions of dollars more.

More GDP Comparisons

The next several tables offer other ways to make relevant points about Chindia and the rest of the developing world, again by looking at their economic output as indicated by GDP. The first, Gross Domestic Product Growth Rates by Region, looks at GDP from the perspective of how quickly it is growing. Note that the High-Income column is a proxy for the developed world, while the Middle-Income and Low-Income columns together constitute the developing world. (Brazil would be an example of a middle-income developing country, while Nigeria and Zimbabwe would be examples of low-income developing countries.) The table also presents GDP growth individually for China, India, and the United States and for the world as a whole.

What does this table show? For one thing, as you can see, since the early 1990s growth rates have been inversely proportional to a nation's income. High-income countries have been the slowpokes in almost every year, while low-income countries have been in the fast lane. Moreover, while the growth rates of rich countries like the United States have been relatively constant, those of poorer nations have been accelerating. This is clear evidence supporting our argument that once capitalism is out of the bag, countries experiencing it want as much as they can get.

Also worth noting is that there are no negative growth rates. While developed nations aren't growing as fast as the developing

Gross Domestic Product Growth Rates by Region (%)

Year	High-Income Countries	Middle-Income Countries	Low-Income Countries	China	India	United States	World
1990	3	1	4	4	6	2	3
1991	1	2	2	9	1	−0	2
1992	2	2	4	14	5	3	2
1993	1	4	4	14	5	3	2
1994	3	4	4	13	7	4	3
1995	3	4	6	11	8	3	3
1996	3	5	7	10	8	4	3
1997	3	6	4	9	4	5	4
1998	2	2	5	8	6	4	2
1999	3	3	6	8	7	4	3
2000	4	6	4	8	4	4	4
2001	1	3	5	8	5	1	2
2002	1	4	4	9	4	2	2
2003	2	5	7	10	8	3	3
2004	3	7	7	10	8	4	4
2005	3	7	8	10	9	3	3
2006	3	7	8	11	9	3	4

Source: World Bank

world, they still are growing. This might, on the surface, seem to lend support to the arguments of some commentators that global growth is a win-win situation for all concerned. We'll come back to this point a little later.

Looking at GDP growth rates tells you how quickly developing nations are climbing the economic ladder, but it doesn't tell you where on the ladder they are. For that, it's more useful to look at per capita GDP, again comparing developing and developed areas and countries. The table Household Final Consumption Expenditures per Capita does just that. As it shows, while growth in the developing world has been outpacing that in the developed world, the developing world still has a long way to go before its individual inhabitants catch up in terms of their material well-being.

There are many different ways to express this huge gap. Perhaps the most striking way is to look at just how much the developing world, representing 85 percent of the world's population, would have to climb merely to reach average world levels of consumption. Middle-income countries would have to nearly triple their consumption. China's consumption would have to rise to between five and six times its current level. And low-income countries, whose overall consumption is less than $1 a day (measured

Household Final Consumption Expenditures per Capita (2000 U.S. Dollars)

Year	High-Income Countries	Middle-Income Countries	Low-Income Countries	China	India	United States	World
1990	13,214	811	223	211	226	19,110	2,778
1991	13,300	823	223	223	226	18,888	2,779
1992	13,561	841	224	251	227	19,238	2,812
1993	13,707	871	227	284	233	19,621	2,836
1994	14,032	894	229	297	239	20,107	2,885
1995	14,238	912	238	328	249	20,405	2,918
1996	14,552	945	248	360	264	20,859	2,973
1997	14,848	979	251	372	265	21,389	3,022
1998	15,173	1,005	258	391	276	22,207	3,072
1999	15,662	1,017	265	417	287	23,074	3,143
2000	16,103	1,053	264	439	290	23,880	3,218
2001	16,369	1,074	271	460	302	24,227	3,257
2002	16,613	1,092	273	489	304	24,640	3,290
2003	16,804	1,129	281	519	320	25,087	3,326
2004	17,168	1,182	292	552	331	25,804	3,399
2005	17,485	1,248	306	595	349	26,445	3,470
2006	..	1,323	317	651	365	..	..

Source: World Bank

in year 2000 dollars), would have to see their consumption climb more than elevenfold.

And that, as we said, is just to reach average levels. To reach the level of high-income countries—never mind that of the United States—the per capita income of middle-income countries would need to rise to fifteen times their current level, while that of low-income countries would need to jump fifty-five times higher!

The next table translates these per capita numbers into gross numbers, and that's when you can really start to appreciate the kinds of pressures on resources that the developing world's drive toward capitalism will entail. The table is titled Total Household Consumption. It shows that if the developing world were to catch up to average world levels—that is, if middle-income countries did in fact triple their consumption and low-income countries increased consumption elevenfold—it would mean that worldwide consumption would need to double. And if developing countries were to achieve the per capita consumption of the high-income world as a whole, total worldwide consumption would be six times greater than in 2005.

Given the constraints on the supplies of energy and other commodities that we've seen already, is it really reasonable to believe this is possible? Clearly, something will have to give long before anything like this improvement in the lot of the developing world is achieved.

To be fair, it's true that consumption patterns do change as an economy grows. Once a country reaches a certain level—once it achieves postindustrial status—services start becoming much more important than manufacturing. At that point, economic growth tends to slow down, and per capita consumption of resources can level off or even decline. However, the chance that the developing world can reach this phase before the arrival of Absolute Peaks is virtually nil.

Total Household Consumption (Billions of Dollars)

Year	High-Income Countries	Middle-Income Countries	Low-Income Countries	China	India	United States	World
1999	15,349	2,947	562	523	287	6,439	18,849
2000	15,907	3,083	570	554	295	6,739	19,552
2001	16,279	3,172	597	585	312	6,910	20,038
2002	16,635	3,257	613	626	318	7,099	20,494
2003	16,955	3,398	644	668	341	7,295	20,982
2004	17,447	3,587	681	715	358	7,577	21,696
2005	17,898	3,820	728	776	382	7,841	22,422
2006	..	4,084	768	855	405	..	..

Source: World Bank

What It All Means for Energy

Finally, let's look directly at how much more energy will be needed by the developing world as it continues to move up the economic ladder. According to the most recent figures from the World Bank, middle-income countries consume about 16 percent less energy per capita than the world's average, while low-income countries consume only one-third the world's average. Compared to high-income countries, middle-income countries consume only about 30 percent as much energy, while low-income countries consume less than one-tenth the energy per capita that high-income countries consume.

Keep these figures in mind when you look at our final table, Absolute Amounts of Energy Consumed. It shows the absolute amounts of energy consumed, measured in millions of kilotons, by the developing and the developed world, by China, India, and the United States, and by the world overall.

If the energy consumption of middle-income and low-income countries rose to the world's average, it would mean a nearly 40

Absolute Amounts of Energy Consumed (Millions of Kilotons)

Year	High-Income Countries	Middle-Income Countries	Low-Income Countries	China	India	United States	World
1999	5.2	3.5	0.9	1.1	0.5	2.2	9.6
2000	5.3	3.6	0.9	1.1	0.5	2.3	9.8
2001	5.3	3.6	1.0	1.1	0.5	2.3	9.9
2002	5.4	3.8	1.0	1.2	0.5	2.3	10.1
2003	5.4	4.0	1.0	1.4	0.5	2.3	10.4
2004	5.6	4.3	1.1	1.6	0.5	2.3	10.9
2005	5.6	4.5	1.1	1.7	0.5	2.3	11.2

Source: World Bank

percent increase in global energy consumption. Assuming the increase was spread equally among the various fossil fuels, the world would be burning 35 million barrels of oil a day more than we do now. And yet according to the best estimates, it is highly doubtful that oil production could be increased by as much as 10 million barrels.

Or even more impossible, imagine what would happen if middle- and low-income countries reached high-income status. The world's energy consumption would be more than three times higher than in 2005. We would be burning roughly 200 million additional barrels of oil a day!

Clearly, the oil isn't there and this isn't going to happen. Long before the developing world reaches parity with the developed world, oil will be largely unavailable. Growth will be able to continue only if we find a way to drastically increase our energy supplies through alternative energies, and even then, limits to other resources eventually will cap growth at some level well below parity.

Meanwhile, though, the pressures for growth continue. The squeeze on oil and other commodities will get worse, and prices will go higher, meaning the world is set to experience growing scarcities of energy and virtually every other commodity, with the inevitable consequence of sharply higher inflation.

Using Their Own Resources

Here's something else to keep in mind. Most of the world's important stores of oil and other resources are found in developing nations. As these nations continue to grow, increasingly they will need to use more of these resources for their own economies, with less to spare to export to the developed world. This will contribute further to shortages and steep price rises in commodities—and hence to overall inflation—as large portions of deposits, in effect, become reserved for the use of the countries whose borders contain them.

If you're wondering, by the way, why it's the poorer, developing nations that now seem to have the greatest reserves of valuable commodities, including oil, while the countries with more money and bigger economies have fewer reserves, it's no coincidence. Rather, it's almost a corollary of human nature. Consider, for example, that Western nations, including the United States, themselves used to be high in natural resources. But we developed and used our resources to make our own economy grow. And actually, we still have a lot of resources; we just don't have much in the way of surplus resources. Instead, our consumption now outpaces our production by a considerable margin.

To understand why, imagine you won a lottery, giving you a guaranteed monthly income of $20,000 for the rest of your life. But unlike most lotteries, instead of automatically taking all the money each month, you can take whatever part of it you want and donate the remainder to charity.

Now maybe there are some altruistic people around who would start out saying, "Oh, I don't need $20,000. I'll do just fine with an extra $5,000. Let the rest go toward making someone else comfortable."

But even these upstanding folk might eventually be tempted to take more of the funds for themselves, to meet unexpected medical costs, say, or renovate their home, or buy a new car. In time, they're likely to feel they need the full amount on a regular basis (which is the attitude most people would have taken from day one). Moreover, if they're typical Americans, they'll likely go a step further. They'll borrow against their income stream, using it to finance loans so that they can improve their lifestyle even more.

The same dynamic is at work with countries and their natural resources. When a nation learns to develop its resources, it puts itself on the path of economic growth. Growth is so rewarding that the nation, eventually, will want to harness its resources to their full capacity, meaning that consumption will expand as much as the available resources allow.

That's what happened in the United States. It has a very high standard of living today because it developed its resources to the fullest. The trouble, though, is that improving your lifestyle is addictive. No one wants to give it up or cut back. So once its own resource production peaks, a nation must look elsewhere for more resources.

For example, in the 1970s, when oil production in the United States reached its peak and started to decline, we started buying more oil from less developed countries. The same thing occurred with metals and other natural resources in which we used to be self-sufficient.

As resources in less developed nations are developed, though, guess what happens? Their economies grow. The people in those nations start to enjoy the benefits of wealth and soon start doing what we did: maximizing their resource production and upgrading their lifestyle. And as they consume more for themselves, they have less to export.

Eventually, the entire world will be in the same situation. Everyone will want more oil, metals, food, and so on, but there will be nowhere left to find them at a reasonable cost. At that point, the world will experience a permanent cap on economic growth.

Incidentally, one implication is that it actually could be a negative for the United States if Middle East nations develop into modern, Western-style economies while we still depend on oil as our major energy source. Suppose that oil reserves in the Middle East are greater than we think likely. It wouldn't do us much good, and it wouldn't help much in putting off Peak Oil, if the oil-producing countries began growing rapidly themselves. For if they did, they would start to need almost all their extra oil for themselves, and they would be willing to sell the rest only at very high prices.

Maybe the World Isn't So Flat?

Before leaving our discussion of the developing world, we want to comment on a point of view that is being propounded by many very bright economists and commentators. They've been looking at the bright side of globalization. They see the developing world joining capitalism's dance and imagine that this process can continue to unfold to the benefit of everyone.

Thomas Friedman views it this way in his recent bestseller *The World Is Flat*. He describes how growth in the developing world is being powered by changes that have leveled the playing field between developing and developed nations, between small and large companies, and even between individuals and institutions. These changes include the fall of communism, the spread of personal computers and the Internet, outsourcing, and the growing cooperation among companies regardless of national borders.

With international borders becoming less relevant, he notes, the entire world has access to resources and tools it never used to have. The United States has access to labor in the developing world, while the developing world has access to the technology, business tools, and markets of the developed world. As a result, Friedman and others argue, the developing world will continue to grow until it enjoys a lifestyle commensurate with that of the developed world.

As Friedman puts it, "what the flattening of the world means is that we are now connecting all the knowledge centers on the planet together into a single global network, which—if politics and terrorism do not get in the way—could usher in an amazing era of prosperity, innovation, and collaboration, by companies, communities, and individuals" (*The World Is Flat: A Brief History of the Twenty-first Century*, version 3.0, Toronto: Douglas & McIntyre, 2007).

And later, he writes: "globalization has a huge potential to lift large numbers of people out of poverty. And when I see large numbers of people escaping poverty in places like India, China, or Ireland, well, yes, I get a little emotional."

Friedman isn't alone in wholeheartedly embracing the idea that economic development, which allows the production of ever more goods, should be a primary goal of humanity and that it is an obtainable goal. But as all the numbers we presented should make plain, global growth simply isn't going to be able to continue indefinitely. There's no way the world as a whole can keep developing until it gets at or close to consumption levels of the developed world. Development takes resources, and there just aren't enough of them to support development on such a gigantic scale.

In our next two chapters we turn our attention away from the developing world to look at one more factor that helps account for the growing imbalances between the demand for oil and other resources and our ability to expand supply. That factor: the burgeoning complexity of our modern world.

CHAPTER 5

The Curse and Cost
of Complexity

Recently someone e-mailed one of us the following, which has been floating around for a while on the Internet and no doubt adorns many a T-shirt as well:

A Little Perspective

- Pythagorean theorem: 24 words
- The Lord's Prayer: 66 words
- Archimedes' principle: 67 words
- The Ten Commandments: 179 words
- The Gettysburg Address: 286 words
- The Declaration of Independence: 1,300 words
- U.S. governmental regulations on the sale of cabbage: 26,911 words

It's an inescapable fact that as civilizations progress, complexity blossoms. In fact, complexity, including ever more detailed governmental regulations on cabbage and everything else, is part and parcel of civilization. Complexity is a two-edged sword. It makes possible the many blessings and comforts of modern life we take for granted—everything from highways to newspapers to indoor plumbing to the corner deli. But as civilizations develop, their growing complexity can take on an increasingly burdensome cast, making everyday transactions more cumbersome and expensive and serving as a drag on progress.

Almost by definition, complexity goes hand in hand with a rising need for energy and other natural resources, which are essential to sustain all the activities of a complex society. We could express this in the obverse way as well: complex civilizations are highly vulnerable to shortages in energy and metals and minerals. History bears this out, offering many examples of complex civilizations that couldn't cope when they ran short of energy and other essential resources.

In today's world, where finding a solution to resource shortages is fast becoming our major challenge, many of complexity's outgrowths are making the job even tougher than it otherwise would be. In particular, by imposing layers of extra costs, they make us less able to find and develop remaining sources of oil and other commodities. Similarly, they make it harder to move ahead with alternative energies.

Complexity costs are far more significant than is generally realized. In chapter 2, we showed how the vicious circle that connects energy, water, and a whole array of metals and minerals is leading to mounting costs for all these commodities. But even if resources were more abundant than they are, their development still would be increasingly burdened by the rising costs that go along with efforts to maintain our increasingly complex society. Because of rising complexity, the costs of finding and developing resources always increase over time. As costs rise, the number of deposits that are economically viable declines. As fewer deposits are developed, it becomes harder for us to meet our growing need for resources, and commodity prices soar.

You might think that since many of complexity's manifestations—our legal system and our financial markets, to name just two—stem from human choice, they should be more malleable than physical limits to resources. But it's not that simple. Trying to peel back many of the complex arrangements that have evolved over time would mean undoing what generations of people have worked to accomplish. Such efforts would run head-on into enormous opposition from a wide range of groups and even from the population at large. Even so, there may be ways to streamline some complexities so as to buy us extra time. We offer a few suggestions in chapter 10, but we wouldn't count on these carrying us through. And at some point, as resource shortages worsen, complexity may simply collapse under its own weight, leading to a simpler society.

For now, though, the reality is that we live in a society of intense complexity, one more factor that contributes to the growing squeeze on energy and other natural resources. In calculating how close we are to Peaks and Absolute Peaks, it's important to understand how complexities burden the search for solutions. In fact, complexity could well be the straw that tips us into Game Over.

History Lessons

We're not the first civilization to suffer from rising complexity in the context of shrinking resources. Let's step back a moment from our present-day dilemmas for some historical perspective.

Human civilization essentially started around 11,500 years ago when a major climate change made agriculture possible for the first time (Peter J. Richerson, "Institutional Evolution in the Holocene: The Rise of Complex Societies," British Academy/ Novartis Foundation meeting on the Origin of Human Social Institutions organized by W. G. Runciman, April 2000. Draft 8/22/00). Human beings, who until then had lived in small tribes of hunter-gatherers, gained the ability to produce and store food, giving humanity its first major increase in energy supplies.

The availability of more food supported larger populations, which led to an increase in available human labor. This surplus of labor allowed a whole range of new occupations and trades to emerge, so that in addition to farmers, society had workers specializing in producing textiles, ceramics, metals, and many other goods and services. Observers as early as Plato noted that such a division of labor is a primary difference between primitive and civilized cultures.

Settled agrarian societies enabled people to accumulate more possessions than they could carry on their backs. The division of labor meant there were many more products that people wanted. The result was an explosion of wealth, which in turn led to new social structures.

In this evolving, more complex civilization, people had to agree on who owned what. Wealth could be amassed, given as a reward to the deserving, passed down to heirs, and collected as taxes. It also could be seized through warfare against neighboring communities. The development of specialized professions and new kinds of merchandise brought markets into existence, and these necessitated new structures, such as money and standardized measurements, to ensure fair exchange as well as the creation of authorities to enforce the rules.

New hierarchies arose, based on wealth, class, education, and military might. And agriculture freed up enough surplus labor to build monumental temples and whole cities. This construction, in turn, engendered organized hierarchies of menials, apprentices, skilled workers, foremen, managers, and architects.

Historians and sociologists consider these two elements—*division of labor* and *hierarchical organization*—to be the defining traits of complex societies. But complex societies are alike in another way: they require access to sufficient energy. In fact, complexity and energy are mutually dependent. Complexity allows societies to develop energy supplies in an efficient manner and, equally true, increases in energy allow societies to develop higher levels of complexity.

Complexity's Downside

As we noted above, though, complexity has its downside. Cyril Parkinson, a literary humorist and close observer of the British Civil Service in the mid-twentieth century, put it this way in his immortal Third Law: "Expansion means complexity and complexity, decay." Complex societies generate ever more complexity in an effort to solve more problems and provide more benefits. But while the number of desired benefits is endless, resources are not. Once the available resources are largely developed, the steady growth of complexity becomes a mounting burden, a superstructure that saps the energies and funds of everyone.

Joseph Tainter, in his book *The Collapse of Complex Societies* (Cambridge University Press, 1988, pp. 91–92), describes this process as follows:

> More complex societies are costlier to maintain than simple ones....As societies increase in complexity, more networks are created among individuals, more hierarchical controls are created to regulate these networks, more information is processed, there is more centralization of information

flow, there is increasing need to support specialists not directly involved in resource production, and the like. All of this complexity is dependent upon energy flow at a scale vastly greater than that characterizing small groups of self-sufficient foragers or agriculturalists. The result is that as a society evolves toward greater complexity, the support costs levied on each individual will also rise, so that the population as a whole must allocate increasing portions of its energy budget to maintaining organizational institutions.

In other words, compared to simpler societies, complex societies must devote a bigger proportion of their overall assets to energy production. Moreover, as societies become more complex, it becomes ever costlier to develop new supplies of energy, as layers of complexity—laws, regulations, taxes—wrap themselves around any new venture. In time, getting more energy simply becomes unaffordable. At that point, the only way for the civilization to survive is by giving up on its complexity. That's what happened to some ancient Mayan communities. Their culture survived only because they devolved into a simpler social order.

More typically, though, *when complex societies run low on resources, they undergo wholesale collapse, usually accompanied by large-scale violence and starvation.* So it was, for instance, with the Roman Empire. By the fifth century C.E., Rome had become the world's most successful civilization ever, dominating most of Europe, North Africa, the Middle East, and parts of Asia. For the most privileged Romans, the empire's complex society conferred a life of great luxury and ease. But over time that complexity became an albatross around its neck.

The primary energy source in ancient Rome was human labor (and agriculture, which produced the food necessary to fuel that human labor). As Roman society became more complex, it required ever more cheap labor (primarily slaves) to sustain it. But the price of adding to the labor force kept rising. As Rome ran out of surplus energy, it became an easy target for invaders. It has been said that the Visigoths and Vandals didn't so much conquer Rome as waltz in and walk over a corpse. Lacking the resources to defend itself, Rome collapsed.

Eventually, after much hardship, Europe developed simpler social structures that offered far fewer benefits to most of its people. Europe endured a thousand years of this relative darkness before the Renaissance bloomed in Italy's city-states, and complexity once again began to expand. Finally, in the eighteenth century, the British industrial revolution and the harnessing of fossil fuels such as coal and oil made possible a new era marked by great energy surpluses. Civilization entered a new phase that took us to heights of complexity and prosperity even the Romans never could have imagined.

Complexity and Oil Production

Today, with resources running low, complexity once again is showing its albatross-like side. Nowhere is this more apparent than in the area of oil production.

A few decades ago, in the days before OPEC, when the United States was self-sufficient in energy, getting a barrel of oil out of the ground was pretty simple. All you had to do was to drill a hole in the right place (and back then there were a lot more right places and they were a lot easier to find), funnel the oil into a truck or railway tank car, ship it to its destination, and bill the buyer for the going price, which in those days was almost completely determined by the policies of the Texas Railroad Commission.

True, it wasn't total bliss. As Daniel Yergin describes in his Pulitzer Prize–winning book *The Prize: The Epic Quest for Oil,*

Money & Power, the absence of regulation during the development of the East Texas region nearly destroyed the U.S. oil industry. Eventually, though, a new set of regulations emerged, providing welcome stability: Yergin writes, "the regulatory system as it finally evolved did indeed possess a powerful underlying logic. It rewrote the book on production and even, to some degree, on what constituted ownership of oil reserves.... Prices themselves were not fixed by the government under the system.... Still setting production levels to match market demand did establish a level of crude output that could be marketed at a stable price."

This regulatory system proved its worth—and showed the beneficial side of complexity—leading to years of stable oil supply that supported much prosperity. But even as oil production in the United States has peaked, complexity has continued to grow, in general and in ways specific to the oil industry. Each dimension of complexity adds to the costs of oil and thus to the costs of other resources as well. Even if—as some argue—technology could help locate big new deposits of oil and minerals, oil prices still would rise over time. That's because complexity would continue to increase. Resource prices would have to remain in a long-term uptrend because producers would need to cover the rising costs of complexity.

The Canadian investment firm BMO has calculated that exploration and production expenditures account for only around 15 percent of oil companies' total costs. The remaining costs come from transportation, depreciation, office salaries, royalties paid to the owner of the land, marketing, legal fees, taxes, and other ancillary items. All these costs are directly related to the world's complexity, which means that as civilization expands we should expect them to continue to rise further. And they all contribute to making it harder and more expensive to get oil out of the ground.

Taxes are arguably the clearest indication of what it costs to run our complex civilization. They pay for government, which provides a host of benefits and services: legal rights; police, military, and the justice system; regulations to ensure fair markets; roads and other infrastructure; trade; a stable currency; and more. And they make possible numerous programs that directly benefit individuals and corporations alike, including unemployment insurance, welfare, schools, Social Security, and Medicare.

But the tax burden also makes it harder to develop new energy supplies. To give one concrete example, the United States today needs to find more natural gas. Alaska is a potential low-cost source, so a pipeline carrying Alaskan natural gas to the continental U.S. should be a profitable venture. Yet ExxonMobil, the world's largest oil company, is on record as saying it won't build such a pipeline because of the uncertain tax situation. ExxonMobil also backed down from a massive gas project in Qatar, again citing a variety of costs, none of which related to exploration and development.

Because of our complex tax system, companies must employ huge numbers of accountants and tax experts to determine how much they owe the government, and not just the U.S. government but also the government in each country where they operate. For multinational corporations in particular, determining a tax bill is an extremely complicated procedure. Not only are the tax laws in each country immensely convoluted, but they're also being constantly rewritten in response to the changing demands of very complex economies and the dictates of various political constituencies. Dealing with this adds considerably to oil companies' overall costs.

(It's true that, on the upside, some companies do receive tax breaks—though these do nothing to reduce complexity but merely shift the burden onto others. Keep in mind, though, that any money not collected from oil companies is money that potentially could have gone to something useful, such as developing alternative energies.)

Complying with government regulations involves a whole other slew of costs, including paying for another raft of employees. And because regulations become more complex and difficult to assess over time, they make it harder for oil companies to calculate future profits.

Environmental regulations, for instance, are one manifestation of our complex civilization—back in the days when life was simpler there were no such things. And while they contribute to people's health and have long-term benefits, they also make it more difficult to deal effectively with energy shortages. Consider, for instance, that the *newest* oil refinery built in the United States was constructed during the mid-1970s. Not surprisingly, our refineries—which are essential for turning oil into useful products such as gasoline, heating oil, jet engine fuel, and more—have been plagued by technical problems. But the obstacles to building new, up-to-date ones are enormous, because refineries emit pollution. Would-be builders must negotiate a complex maze of environmental regulations to get approval, as well as overcome "not in my backyard" sentiment.

We said before that we're facing tough choices and trade-offs. As resource shortages worsen and prices rise, choices that today might seem unthinkable might well come to seem sensible—indeed, essential if we are to survive. At the very least, a lot more will be on the table than is currently the case.

In the next chapter we continue our look at complexity by seeing how one of the most convoluted products of our complex society—Wall Street—directly, and negatively, burdens the search for more resources and alternative energies.

CHAPTER 6

Wall Street, Complexity, and the Shortfall in Resources

B efore the 1970s, the stock market and brokerage firms had very little to do with the production and marketing of oil. Today, however, there is no better example of the exponential growth of complexity and its associated costs than the many ways in which Wall Street complicates and inhibits the development of oil supplies. The opinions of stock analysts today are as important as those of geologists in determining which new oil projects will get a green light and which get shelved. Naturally, similar dynamics apply to the alternative energy industry and to natural resource ventures other than oil. However, to keep things simple, let's look in particular at Wall Street's contribution to the growing crisis in the oil industry.

Focusing on the Short Term

The reason for Wall Street's influence, of course, is money. Oil companies, like any other, depend on financing for any sizable venture, and when it comes to money, Wall Street is the place to go.

In particular, companies have a lot more options when their share price is going up. A higher share price means greater access to capital. For instance, the higher the share price, the more money a company can raise if it decides to issue new shares. Higher share prices also tend to imply higher bond ratings, lowering the company's costs of borrowing money. So naturally, companies seek to win investors' favor. Investors, though, rely largely on the brokerage industry to tell them whether a company is a good bet or not. Thus companies strive to convince Wall Street that they are on point and, specifically, that they can generate an acceptable level of earnings growth.

Unfortunately, one direct effect of its burgeoning complexity is that Wall Street today tends to take a short-term, cover-your-own-back perspective in evaluating companies. This wasn't always true. As recently as the 1980s, Wall Street analysts operated with far more independence than today, making it fairly simple for an analyst to issue a buy or sell recommendation. An analyst began by researching a particular stock or industry. If he liked what he saw, he wrote a favorable report and sent it out to his clients. A client could pay a direct fee for each report or could agree to trade stocks through the analyst's brokerage firm, in which case part of the commissions helped cover research costs. The arrangement could be per year or per report. There was a lot of flexibility and a lot of independence.

Of course, our analyst had to follow some rules. If he owned the stock he recommended, he couldn't sell it immediately after issuing the buy report. That would be fraud, and the U.S. Securities and Exchange Commission (SEC) could put him out of business. But overall the rules weren't too onerous or hard to follow.

Look at a typical stock report today, though, and you'll see how times have changed. It will contain reams of language disclosing the brokerage house's relationship with the company being covered. It will note, for example, whether or not the firm has a position in the underlying stock, and it will state that the information in the report and the conclusions have been approved by the company for whom the analyst works. There will be a history of past recommendations on the same stock and a statement of risk. For instance, if the report recommends buying an oil stock, it will caution the reader that if oil prices go down more than expected, the share price might fall, too. A recent report on General Electric from a major Wall Street firm even took pains to state that "failure to execute a strategy" was a risk!

Investors who buy these reports pay for a lot of words they probably don't bother to read. Moreover, and not so incidentally, producing these reports has direct costs to society, including significant extra energy usage in the form of the endless pages of paper used up, the computers and printers that must be operated, and so on.

And that's just the start. The caveats in the report, however obvious, not only have to be written down, they have to be sworn to. The analyst whose name goes on the report has to certify that his views are accurately reflected—that is, he isn't deliberately lying. The firm must maintain a well-paid legal team in case some investor, saying he relied on the report, buys the stock, loses money, and decides to sue. Unless the firm is a one-man shop, the analyst must get approval from his superiors for all the statements in the report.

One reason making a simple stock recommendation requires so many layers of red tape is that, in another manifestation of rising complexity, today most Wall Street firms wear at least two hats. On the one hand, they carry out research that is supposed to be independent and unbiased. On the other, they are investment bankers, raising money for companies by issuing and selling securities. The potential for a conflict of interest is obvious should the firm decide to recommend a company that pays it handsome sums to serve as its investment banker. These rules are intended to protect investors, and they also protect the firms against those disgruntled investors referred to above who might choose to bring legal action (thereby activating yet another arena of awesome complexity, our legal system). *But the upshot, with respect to oil companies, has been to throw roadblocks in the way of many projects with the potential to add to oil production and reserves down the road.* And the same goes for alternative energy projects, too.

That's because, with all these steps and approvals and bureaucratic layers that come into play in issuing a single report, caution is likely to rule the day. What most impresses Wall Street these days are companies that can produce consistent earnings growth, quarter after quarter. With sizable oil fields getting harder to find, that's no easy task for oil companies, which are becoming increasingly hard-pressed to raise production. But ironically, the need to please Wall Street makes it even less likely oil companies will boost production, because they are fearful of investing in any project about which Wall Street has any doubts. So they are likely to refrain from taking a chance on a project that might hurt profits in the shorter term even if the longer-term prospects are promising.

For instance, suppose an oil executive believes oil prices will remain in a long-term uptrend—that they will likely top $200 a barrel by the end of the decade and continue to rise from there. If he were right, it would make a lot of sense to invest in a project likely to produce oil at the cost of $100 a barrel. But Wall Street—which currently assumes that oil prices will fall to where over the longer term they average $85 to $90 a barrel—would consider such a project a huge gamble. It would generate negative research that would punish the oil company's stock and make it difficult to fund the project.

Investors' expectations are another stumbling block in the path of new oil projects. Before oil executives can decide whether to proceed with a project, they must be confident the profits will satisfy their shareholders. These days, shareholders generally expect a return of around 15 percent a year. If oil were selling at $85 a barrel and the total costs of a project were expected to equal $80 a barrel, only $5 profit would be left for shareholders—not nearly enough. Such a project would be shelved, at least until oil prices rose to higher levels.

And speaking of shareholders, whom companies need to woo both directly and via brokerage houses, Wall Street's growing complexity has engendered in them an unhealthy emphasis on short-term results. Much of the blame goes to the personal computer, which, like Wall Street itself, is both a product of complexity and an agent that increases it further. Why are personal computers culprits here? Because by offering individuals access to online trading and automatic trading programs, they have turned millions of investors into short-term "players," or traders. In the 1960s, the typical investor held on to a stock for about five years and viewed the shares as representing part ownership in a company. Today, too many people view shares as nothing more than pieces of paper to trade. They often know little about the companies they invest in and feel no attachment to them. Consequently, the average holding period for positions is down to just ten months.

When shareholders lack a long-term commitment to a company, managers feel even more pressure to push earnings up quarter after quarter. Managers who fail to do so may find themselves out of a job. Whether they like it or not, they are forced to pursue short-term results rather than create long-term value.

Commenting on this trend, *BusinessWeek* columnists Clayton M. Christensen and Scott D. Anthony wrote in 2007: "Well-intentioned, smart managers are systematically destroying companies by failing to take actions they know are right in the long term. Instead of slavishly serving an antiquated and increasingly irrelevant function, managers should find ways to reward investors and stakeholders who want innovation, not plunder" ("Put Investors in Their Place," May 28, 2007: 108).

To sum up: in our complex financial system, oil companies depend on Wall Street's favorable opinion. But the effort to obtain it places a burden on oil companies that, far more than is generally recognized, complicates their decision-making, pushes costs higher, and makes more projects viable only at higher oil prices. Adding insult to injury, in recognition of Wall Street's clout, oil companies along with all other public companies need to devote considerable resources to investor relations, another incremental cost that gets translated into the calculus of how high oil prices must be to make new projects worthwhile.

Traders and Speculators

As we said above, oil executives need to have a good idea where oil prices will be in the future so that, before committing huge sums to any new project, they can be confident it will be profitable. Projecting prices might seem like basic economics, a question of supply and demand (although predicting even those variables leaves plenty of room for error). But nothing is simple on Wall Street anymore. As a result, many other factors come into play that make accurate projections nearly impossible.

For starters, like most commodities, oil is traded on both a spot and a futures market. The spot market tells you what prices are at that moment, while the futures market is a bet on where oil prices will be on a particular date in the future. The futures markets, for oil and other commodities, arose as a means of helping producers manage cash flow. By agreeing to sell some or all of their future production at an agreed-upon price, producers can hedge their bets and make their earnings more predictable. Obviously, in the case of oil producers, if oil rises above the price set in the futures contract, they won't get all the benefits; on the other hand, if oil prices drop, they don't lose.

In theory, the price of oil on the futures market represents a best guess as to where oil will be trading when the contracts come due. Complicating matters, though, is that the actual economic participants—oil producers and buyers of oil—aren't the only entities involved in the futures markets. There also are the speculators, those infamous players who became such a dirty word as oil prices soared. Speculators don't take possession of oil for their own use; they simply buy and sell futures contracts. The appeal for them is that futures contracts permit the purchase of future oil production on margin. For instance, for an investment of $1,000, they can buy $10,000 worth of oil to be delivered at a future date, when the contracts come due. Because the margin requirements are so low, speculators can rake in leveraged profits as profits change.

Of course, in order to make money, speculators need to be on the right side of oil's moves. To project where oil is headed, they rely on a whole array of short-term predictive tools, from trend lines to elaborate analyses of supply and demand relationships. The point, though, is that they're not just making predictions. Rather, their actions in themselves influence how oil prices will move, because a whole slew of investors who follow the oil market pay close attention to what the speculators are doing.

For example, if speculators' technical tools tell them that oil is going up, and they bid accordingly, many investors who watch their every move may similarly believe oil is headed higher and will be big buyers of oil company stocks. Rising oil shares could then further affect oil futures. At some point, despite speculation, oil and other commodity prices do gravitate toward their real economic value. That's because the end users of a commodity, not the speculators, are the ones who ultimately take possession. In other words, the last purchase of a commodity on a futures exchange will be made by someone who needs the commodity and believes the asking price is reasonable. Nonetheless, speculators can create a lot of volatility over the short term, making it very difficult to see what the real economic price is.

Further volatility is created by the short-term traders in the shares of oil companies. Such traders buy or sell according to computer models based on instantaneous and longer-term disparities between where the stock is and where the model says it should be. Let's suppose, for example, that these traders notice that shares of Exxon, the world's largest oil company, move in step with changes in oil prices. Let's further suppose that, historically, these changes are within a consistent range—for instance, that when oil moves up 1 percent, Exxon shares also move up no more than 1 percent higher than some other number. Then, if oil moves up 1 percent and Exxon shares jump outside the expected range—and there are no outside factors to explain the discrepancy—the traders would hop onto the divergence and sell. If the stock price dropped below the expected range, they would buy. All these actions create further volatility.

The actions both of speculators in oil futures and traders in oil shares create a situation where oil prices respond more to changing short-term perceptions than to actual long-term changes in supply and demand. This results in higher volatility and an increased risk of severe market reactions. No wonder it is so hard for oil executives to figure out where oil will be at any future time.

So, as some in the political arena have argued, should we take action against the speculators? No, because in today's complex world they are necessary to ensure the smooth functioning of the system. *For all the complaints made against speculators, they supply necessary liquidity to the market.* They virtually guarantee that whenever an economic participant wants to buy or sell, there will be someone on the other side who'll sell or buy at some price.

Still, it isn't hard to sympathize with those who see speculators as reaping unfair benefits. Speculators can make a ton of money (of course, they can lose big, too, if they're on the wrong side of big moves). In 2006, the person who had the largest income in the world for the year was a speculator: James Simons. He made nearly $2 billion thanks to his huge computer network programmed to take advantage of disparities among commodities and stocks.

That's a detail, though. The big picture with respect to Wall Street's role is that the Street's demands and expectations have come to dominate much of the decision-making process of companies today, an especially negative trend with respect to oil and other natural resource companies and alternative energy companies. Wall Street's prominent role has become a case of the tail wagging the dog, but there seems little likelihood that the dog will take control again. The financial markets, which developed as a means of enabling companies to grow and flourish, will continue to be a significant factor in keeping energy and other commodity prices high.

PART II

MEETING THE CHALLENGE

CHAPTER 7

We Never Said It
Would Be Easy

In 2007, the U.S. government devoted $4.5 billion to energy research, a stunningly low number. Just consider that in each of the first four years of the Iraq war we spent far more than that on the war *every two months*. In fact, certain individuals—Warren Buffett and Bill Gates spring to mind—could, if they wanted, spend $4.5 billion every year for a decade and still qualify as among the richest individuals on the planet. This pitiful sum shows that, for all the recent talk about the need for energy alternatives, we haven't begun to grasp how urgent the problem is.

We are in a race against time. Developing and switching to alternative energies quickly and on a grand scale must become our top priority. It's our only hope of undoing, before it's too late, the vicious circle of rising scarcities and higher prices afflicting oil and a wide range of essential commodities simultaneously. The longer we wait, the harder the job will become, and if we wait too long, to where we hit Absolute Peak Oil and Absolute Peak Commodities, it will be Game Over.

That's why accomplishing the transition to alternative energies can't be a distant goal, or just one of many competing goals. It trumps everything, because without a society based on alternative energies, we won't have the capability to deal with anything else, whether combating terrorism or improving our education system or solving the crises in Social Security and Medicare. But if we succeed in this momentous transition, we'll emerge in a much stronger position to deal effectively with all the other problems we face.

Manhattan Project on Steroids

Some people argue that market forces can accomplish this on their own. When oil prices get high enough, these people say, the profit motive will impel companies to get into alternative energy in a big way. So the government doesn't need to get involved, it just needs to get out of the way.

But we don't think there's a prayer that market forces can carry us far along this path on their own. The multiplicity of shortages makes the quest for a solution like trying to solve an unimaginably convoluted Rubik's Cube, where when one side clicks into place, the other sides all fall to the ground. The private sector must be involved and can contribute in a big way, but the profit motive itself won't be enough to provide the overall framework that is so essential.

In other circles it has become almost a cliché to say we need to launch an all-out government-funded effort akin to the Manhattan Project, which developed the atomic bomb. We agree completely—as long as it's recognized that the effort will need to be considerably bigger, more complicated, and more expensive than the Manhattan Project. To succeed, it must encompass two parts, each of which is essential and each of which will involve big dollars.

The first is research. Unlike the Manhattan Project, however, it won't be a question of racing to bring a brand-new technology to fruition, although technological improvements in existing alternative energies could help. *Rather, research must focus on figuring out what combination of existing alternative energies has the greatest long-term potential given the rising shortages of the commodities on which those energies will depend.* And it must factor in the reality that these shortages will accelerate rapidly as the alternative energies that require them become implemented on a large scale.

To put it differently, we need research that looks at the big picture. Otherwise, we risk pursuing projects that at first blush might seem to be winning solutions but that are unsustainable over the longer term, because the resources they depend upon will become unavailable or unaffordable as time goes on. Even worse, we'd be consuming precious stores of finite resources that later on would be unavailable for energies with true long-term potential. We need to act, but we need to act wisely, not in a scattershot way.

To do this, we need to bring together the best scientists, geologists, mathematicians, economists, and others capable of collecting and analyzing data and looking in a rigorous way at the interrelationships among essential resources, including oil, metals and minerals, and water. We need to set clear goals and provide whatever funding is required—and do all this with a sense of urgency.

That's the first part. The second part is building the extensive new infrastructure that inevitably will be required, along with reconfiguring existing infrastructure. Like the research effort, this will take massive sums of money and must be national in scope. It should be coming clear why the private sector can't begin to do all this on its own, any more than last century it could have built the nation's vast system of interstate highways.

In all, making the transition to alternative energies will cost in the trillions of dollars. But there is no way to skirt it. Without such a large-scale commitment by government, we will be incapable of moving away from oil in time to avert Game Over. That's why we think it's a question of when, not if, such huge outlays will be made. These will be one more factor that will push inflation to new heights in coming years. (Of course, if we're wrong—that is, if we fail to make such a national commitment to implementing renewable energies—inflation is still likely to maintain its jagged rise to new levels as the oil and other commodities upon which we depend continue to become ever scarcer.)

We Must Overcome

It's easy to say we must do all the above. But obstacles to action lurk everywhere, both around us and within us. We need to know what these roadblocks are if we're to have a chance of overcoming them so as to make the switch to alternative energies in time.

Our complex civilization makes it difficult to take prompt, effective action on almost anything. Gridlock in Congress, partisan politics, a multitude of interest groups and lobbyists, endless regulations, state-federal jurisdictional conflicts, Wall Street's insistence on short-term payoffs, "not in my backyard" outcries, our judicial system—the list of why action is hard goes on and on. Most of these complexities aren't going to be rolled back in the near future. But conceivably, there might be ways to streamline some of them—for instance, simplifying some of the jurisdictional questions relating to federal vs. state prerogatives—and doing so should also be part of any concerted effort to enact alternative energies on a grand scale.

Compounding, or perhaps more accurately underlying, the problem of our continuing dependence on oil as our main energy source is the very human trait of denial, the tendency to think that things can't be as bad as, in fact, they really are. Denial goes hand in hand with the equally human tendency to be reluctant to make big changes until forced to do so.

And as time goes on and resource shortages worsen, the impact on the economy will grow. An economic backdrop of rising inflation punctuated by possible recessions, all in the context of high government debt, will make it that much harder to find the political will to fund a big alternative energy effort.

One more roadblock deserves mention, and while it might seem esoteric, it's really important: it's what we call tunnel vision among scientists and other professionals. In our complex society, science has become segmented into narrow specialties, a trend identified more than a decade ago by Peter Galison, a Harvard philosophy of science professor. In his book *Image and Logic* (University of Chicago Press, 1997), Galison noted that each area of science has its own language and set of symbols. Even scientists in areas that are closely related—organic and nonorganic chemistry, for instance—have problems sharing their findings. The problems are compounded many times when it comes, say, to chemists talking to biologists.

Stephen Hawking is considered by many to be the greatest physicist of at least the past generation, but even he has shown himself to be unaware of important developments in physics outside his own specialty. In a book review in the July 31, 2008, issue of *Nature*, Paul Davies notes: "The momentous conclusion that a black hole swallows and permanently obliterates physical information didn't bother Hawking, whose background was in gravitational theory and space-time geometry rather than particle and quantum physics." In other words, Hawking was arguing for something that, if true, would have undermined a vital component of quantum mechanics: the premise that information cannot be destroyed. Yet Hawking, as brilliant as he is, didn't see that this would be the implication—and this was within the field of physics. How aware, then, would you expect Hawking or any other physicist to be of basic principles of chemistry or geology?

The same situation exists outside the physical sciences as well. It sometimes seems, for instance, as if macro- and microeconomists inhabit different planets, for they talk in completely different terms. Even if you look only at economists with a mathematical orientation, there still are deep divisions. Microeconomists focus on highly theoretical applications, while the macro guys focus on statistics and computer programming. It's the rare bird indeed who can bridge the gap between the applied and the abstract.

The social sciences, too, are increasingly fragmented into narrow specialties that know little about one another. The well-known Yale economist Robert Shiller, writing in the *New York Times* on Sunday, August 10, 2008, makes the following observation about the chaos in the financial system that might have resulted if Bear Stearns had been allowed to go into bankruptcy. Recall that Bear Stearns was a major brokerage house that in the wake of subprime losses was bailed out by the Federal Reserve and JPMorgan. Shiller writes:

> Preventing Bear Stearns from becoming the responsibility of the bankruptcy courts was one reason the Fed felt it had to act so quickly. Current bankruptcy law was not written with the perspective of systemic risk in mind. There is a big problem—a discontinuity in macroeconomic outcomes—when large financial institutions are at the margin between solvency and insolvency. The formal declaration that an important financial institution is insolvent could threaten the whole economy.

Bankruptcy law, in other words, was written and is interpreted from a microeconomic point of view, something wholly unrelated to macroeconomic issues. This disconnect, of course, results from our highly complex society, where it is nearly impossible for macro- and microeconomic policies to mesh into a seamless whole. Yet mesh they must if we are going to organize a research and infrastructure project able to solve the energy crisis that we face.

Tunnel vision by scientists, economists, and mathematicians needs to be recognized and addressed, because to launch any sort of effective nationwide system of alternative energies, we will need to recruit and bring together an array of experts in all these areas. No one person, no matter how brilliant, has enough knowledge or information to make such determinations on his or her own, and no one specialty has all the answers. In assembling a research project to sort out the interrelationships among different critical resources and how they relate to the economy, the development of a common language may be one of the most difficult tasks.

These are some of the obstacles, and they are considerable. But human beings have accomplished incredible things in the face of daunting obstacles before. The first essential step is to recognize how urgent the need to develop alternative energies is so that we become utterly committed to mobilizing all our forces to find answers. We have no doubt that we can do this. The question is, *will we do it in time?*

CHAPTER **8**

Alternative Energies

J ust about every day there is an article in some newspaper or another about a seemingly hopeful development related to alternative energies. In Utah, people are rushing to retrofit cars to run on natural gas rather than gasoline. T. Boone Pickens, who knows a thing or two about the oil economy, is launching a 700-turbine wind farm in Texas as part of a push to promote natural gas–fueled cars. New York's Mayor Michael Bloomberg wants to explore putting wind turbines on skyscraper rooftops. Even the Style Section of the *New York Times* recently got in the act with an article about small designer wind turbines for individual homes.

This is all well and good. With oil and gasoline prices having soared to new heights, alternative energies are gaining new prominence and drawing new converts. But if we get too starry-eyed about these pockets of alternative energy activity and think they will effortlessly spread to where oil loses its grip on us, we'll only be misleading ourselves.

There are two key questions to consider in evaluating the true potential of any oil alternative. And no surprise—both relate to the vicious circle that links energy inextricably to other natural resources.

The first question: Does the alternative energy being considered produce a net energy gain? As we've seen, it takes energy to get energy. But in calculating accurately exactly how much energy it takes, you need to account for *all* the energy that must be expended, not just the most direct energy inputs. If you're looking at gasified coal, for instance, you need to factor in the energy used both in mining and in transporting the coal. You also must take into account the energy applied to extracting and transporting the materials for building the gasification plants, along with the energy used to run the plants, and you have to consider the energy that goes into storage facilities. These are very complex equations.

The second question: Besides energy, what other scarce natural resources go into particular alternative energies, and how available and affordable will these be if the alternative energy were implemented on a scale large enough to wean us off oil? In other words, it's essential to realize that there's a huge gap between relatively small forays into alternative energies and the massive national effort necessary to convert us to alternative energies on a meaningful scale.

For instance it's one thing to put up one wind turbine or even hundreds. *But to build the many hundreds of thousands needed to convert our economy to wind energy might require more steel than we have or can get.* Similarly, a natural gas–fueled car might reduce oil use and be better for the environment as well. But if we tried to replace our entire fleet of vehicles with cars that run on natural gas, we'd run out of the fuel in a fairly short period of time. And meanwhile, we'd have squandered resources building the cars and the infrastructure they require.

Unfortunately, this key point is one that even the best-motivated commentators generally miss. A good example is Thomas L. Friedman in his latest book, *Hot, Flat, and Crowded: Why We Need a Green Revolution—and How It Can Renew America* (Farrar, Straus and Giroux, 2008). In it he passionately urges that we commit to developing renewable energies. He gets it half right. But unfortunately, one half without the other is a recipe for danger.

On page 40, Friedman extensively quotes Klaus Kleinfeld, president of aluminum producer Alcoa. Kleinfeld notes:

> Everything today is in shortage—steel, bauxite, construction equipment, engineers, contractors, ships.... You run into bottlenecks everywhere you turn...there are more people on the planet every day and, particularly in the developing world, more of them are moving to urban areas, where they live in high-rise buildings, drive cars or motor scooters, ride buses, fly on airplanes, and start to drink Coke from cans. All of that increases global demand for aluminum. Companies like Alcoa then go out and try to acquire more bauxite. That requires more mines and smelters, and that requires more ships and more steel and more energy, and that requires more engineers and more contractors.

This mirrors much of what we've been describing about the interconnectedness of commodities.

Friedman, too, buys into the view that resources are highly interconnected. But instead of seeing why this is a danger, he takes it as an imperative to develop alternative energies—while failing to see that these alternatives also involve resources. His erroneous assumption seems to be that these resources will be available in whatever quantity we need them.

For example, the book contains not a single mention of Peak Oil. Nor is there any consideration of the possibility that other resources might become so scarce as to preclude the building of an alternative energy infrastructure. On the same page in which he quotes Kleinfeld, he refers to a *Wall Street Journal* article noting that the shortage of steel has been instrumental in slowing down and raising the cost of energy exploration. Yet he does not mention that this shortage stems from the shortage of iron ore—a mineral that between 2004 and 2008 appreciated more than oil.

Later, on page 325, Friedman comments: "Solar and wind power may be more expensive to install today, but the price of the fuel—sun and wind—are fixed. They will be free forever." He then goes on to note that fossil fuels are headed upward in price. He fails to recognize, though, that it's not the abundance of sun and wind that's in question—the problem is that the costs of harnessing these energy sources are also rising sharply over time. And indeed, there may come a time when we just don't have the resources to develop them.

Friedman's book does a great service in pointing out the utter necessity of developing alternative energies. But in glossing over the current obstacles that exist, in the form of the interconnected shortages in many key resources, he makes it seem as though the task will be a lot easier to accomplish than is the case. The risk here is that this will only encourage further complacency.

Below and in the next chapter, we review the major potential oil substitutes and look at some of the pluses and minuses of each. In particular, we zero in on the resources that each requires and suggest the potential trade-offs that each form of energy would entail if implemented on a large scale.

We hope you don't think the discussion is too negative, for we're aware that while on the one hand we're urging a massive commitment to developing alternative energies, on the other we're pointing out drawbacks to each particular candidate. But we're not trying to be naysayers, nor do we want to rule out—or propound—any particular alternative to oil. That's the whole point: there is no one clear-cut answer yet because we don't have enough information. Rather, we're simply raising the kinds of questions that must be asked as part of the massive national or even international effort that is so essential. The dialogue must get started and the right kinds of questions must be raised before real progress is possible.

The Other Fossil Fuels

We often run into optimists who say we're way too glum when it comes to worrying about oil. After all, they point out, if nothing else, the world contains vast reserves of tar sands and oil shale with enough oil to provide us with energy for generations to come. Not to mention, they add, our extensive coal resources. Even if existing coal plants are admittedly dirty, these optimists argue, we should be able to implement clean coal technologies such as coal gasification that will give us more than enough time to develop renewable energies. So even if it's true that conventional oil supplies are indeed getting scarcer, why do we need to get so worked up about these issues right now? Why talk about trillions of dollars in spending on research and infrastructure when we still have access to so much energy in the form of other fossil fuels? Especially when these resources have the supreme merit of being located either in the United States itself or in friendly, politically stable Canada?

Are they right? Could we solve our problems simply by launching a massive program to develop tar sands, shale, and coal? It's not likely. Let's start with tar sands. As soon as we tried to develop them on a large scale, we'd run right into constraints from other commodities, starting with water scarcity. As we noted earlier, processing tar sands requires enormous amounts of water, which is used, among other things, in heating the sands to a very high temperature, a necessary step in separating out the oil. A second constraint is energy: processing the sands is highly energy-intensive. Thus, as energy prices have risen, so have the costs of extracting oil from tar sands.

Moreover, while tar sands advocates often like to say that the sands constitute an energy resource equal to or greater than all the oil in Saudi Arabia, this seems unlikely. Estimates of potential production from the sands have remained remarkably constant at around 2 million to 3 million barrels of oil a day, or about twice the current production. *In other words, the tar sands are unlikely to add more than 1 million to 2 million barrels of oil a day over the next decade.* This wouldn't begin to meet the needs of global growth, while at the same time it would be siphoning off huge amounts of oil and water that might be more profitably used elsewhere.

Still, this is more oil than we are likely to get from shale. Shale has always been the fossil fuel of the future and always will be—that is, its day will never come. A big drawback to shale is that its primary ingredient is kerogen, which is several more degrees removed from oil than is bitumen, the primary ingredient in tar sands. Processing kerogen into oil requires even more water and energy than is needed to process bitumen. As water scarcities become more evident and energy prices rise further, it will become increasingly clear that shale has little potential to replace oil in any meaningful way.

Yet another constraint that applies to both kerogen and bitumen is that once they've been processed, each requires a great deal of refining before it becomes usable. This refining process depends upon hydrogen. The world has plenty of hydrogen—in fact, it's the most abundant element in the universe. The problem is that, in its natural state, hydrogen is always found bonded to other elements; hydrogen and oxygen, for example, bond to make water.

It is possible to "crack" water, obtaining pure hydrogen, but the world wouldn't gain much, as doing this requires the input of a lot of energy. It's easier to get hydrogen from natural gas, which right now is the most abundant source of accessible hydrogen. But natural gas itself is a finite resource, and the more that is devoted to refining kerogen and bitumen, the less that will be available for other purposes.

The bottom line is that while it's feasible to produce relatively small quantities of oil products from bitumen and possibly even from kerogen, we can't keep scaling up the amounts. Even the 2 million to 3 million barrels a day of oil that we said might be the upper limits to what we can get from tar sands—in itself not all that significant an amount—may exceed our capacity.

Coal runs into the same constraints as both tar sands and oil shale: processing it requires plenty of energy and water. Moreover, there is a growing school of thought that our coal resources may be a lot less abundant than is generally assumed. Canadian geologist David Hughes, for instance, has argued that in terms of the BTUs coal can produce, Peak Coal has already occurred in the forty-eight states. That is, while we've used up less than half the coal in the ground, meaning a tremendous amount of coal still is left, this remaining coal has a significantly lower "energy content" than the coal we've mined so far. If true, this would mean that the costs of coal energy will start rising dramatically, because we will have to obtain larger quantities simply to get the same amount of energy.

This argument gains support from the fact that, over the past four years, coal prices have been steeply uptrended, suggesting that coal is less plentiful than the consensus would have it. In fact, as the chart shows, since the middle of this decade, coal prices actually have risen faster than oil prices. Today coal is priced at the equivalent of oil at $60 to $65 a barrel. This, however, doesn't take into account the health costs associated with coal, which could add an extra $10 to the actual costs. If coal prices continue to rise faster than oil prices, the gap will keep narrowing, and if we attempted to turn to coal in a bigger way as a substitute for oil, it would happen a lot faster.

Finally, these fossil fuels cause a lot of damage to the environment. Arguably, no mining process is as dirty as that for tar sands, which contain tremendous amounts of carbon and waste materials such as sulfuric acid. Beyond degrading the environment, the processing of tar sands poses health hazards to individuals, with particulates from the sands leading to a variety of lung diseases.

Oil and Coal Prices, Indexed to January 2003

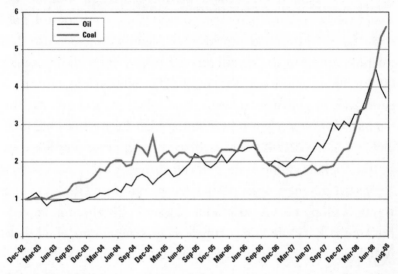

Source: Bloomberg

These are terrible in human terms and must be taken into account when calculating tar sands' economic costs as well, since they add significantly to spending on health care.

Coal, too, is a very dirty fuel. Mining it degrades the physical environment, while burning it contributes in a big way to global warming. And while it's true that coal gasification is a viable technology that allows coal to be burned more cleanly, it becomes clear, when you look at the numbers, that it's not likely to ever replace oil on a large scale.

Consider that right now it costs around $2.5 billion to construct one coal gasification plant that generates 1,000 megawatts of power. As of 2005, the United States was using approximately 4 trillion kilowatt hours of power a year. This means we would need to build 1,200 coal gasification plants to generate all our electricity from coal. (We're assuming we would not be replacing older coal plants, which now provide us with around half of our electricity, with new clean-coal plants.) In today's dollars, the total cost of constructing the new plants would be $1.2 trillion. But that much new construction would vastly tax other resources, which would send construction costs higher. Moreover, to provide those plants with coal feedstocks, we'd have to boost the overall amount of coal we burn by around 60 percent, which we doubt is possible. The bottom line is that coal gasification might satisfy some incremental needs for electricity. But it won't work as a major substitute for other fossil fuels. One final problem with coal is that coal needs to be transported long distances by truck or rail, adding to the drain on energy.

Health and environmental studies don't exist for oil shale, as far as we know, simply because so little oil shale mining has been attempted. But we think it's safe to say that the large-scale mining of oil shale would raise major environmental and health concerns as well.

Nuclear Power

Nuclear power accounts for around 20 percent of U.S. electricity generation today and around 8 percent of our total energy consumption. Decades ago nuclear power was viewed as a safe, clean energy that would be the wave of the future. But it fell out of favor following the near meltdown at the Three Mile Island nuclear power plant in Pennsylvania, and the building of new plants stagnated. Now, though, as oil supplies falter and oil prices rise, nuclear energy is going through a new spurt of respectability and growth worldwide. China has commissioned dozens of plants, and many supporters see nuclear energy as the only here-and-now energy source that can realistically take over the job of supplying us with enough power.

But nuclear power, too, runs into many troubling constraints— starting, as so often is the case, with water. Nuclear power plants require a lot of water for cooling purposes. It's true that most of this water is recycled, not actually used up. But still, any water devoted to cooling nuclear power plants becomes unavailable for drinking, agriculture, and other essential uses. Moreover, the need for water means that nuclear power plants must be built near a water supply, and there aren't all that many suitable sites available, another way in which water serves as a constraint.

Finally, some water used in plants does become contaminated and thus is permanently taken out of circulation, shrinking the world's overall allotment. While these amounts are relatively insignificant now, they would become multiplied many times over if nuclear energy took over in a big way. In a world whose population is expanding and whose needs for freshwater are growing, this is a trade-off that must be taken into account.

In some parts of the world, nuclear power has been explicitly rejected largely because of its huge call on water. Australia, for instance, won't build nuclear plants because the country faces chronic drought and has to watch every drop of water it uses. For the same reason, we wouldn't expect to see a nuclear power plant built anywhere near Atlanta, where lack of water has become a huge problem.

Of course, if we could expand our supply of freshwater by desalinating water from the ocean, none of this would apply. But this brings us back to that fundamental and frustrating vicious circle we discussed earlier: desalinating seawater requires energy and metals; getting energy requires water and metals; and getting metals requires energy and water (and other metals).

Water is only one of several problems we'd face if we tried to rapidly expand our nuclear energy capacity. Another constraint is the need to obtain sufficient quantities of uranium, the basic feedstock for nuclear plants. Uranium used to be very cheap and widely available. But that has changed dramatically this decade. Between 2001 and mid-2007, uranium prices rose more than twentyfold, far faster than oil. The metal did correct sharply after that. But if we tried to boost the world's nuclear capacity enough to transcend growing oil scarcities, the resulting sharp increase in demand for uranium would once again send prices way back up. Indeed, uranium would be hit with a double whammy: the rising demand from nuclear plants plus the rising costs of mining that will result from higher energy prices.

And, of course, nuclear energy still has to contend with major issues of safety that don't come into play with any other form of energy. For one thing, radioactive used nuclear material needs to be contained, and all efforts to do so fight some basic laws of physics. That's because radioactivity is the result of the so-called strong force, the strongest of the four forces that govern the universe, the other three being the electromagnetic force, the weak force, and gravity. The strong force is about a hundred times stronger than the electromagnetic force, which is the one that holds most objects, including human beings, together. Storing radioactive materials involves trying to trick nature in order to contain something stronger in a weaker container. It can't be completely done. In the debate over Yucca Mountain, the United States has struggled for years to try to come to an agreement about where nuclear waste can be safely stored.

Further, there is the risk that radioactive materials could be stolen and used by terrorists or rogue countries to make nuclear weapons. The more nuclear power plants that are built, the greater such concerns will become, and the more attention and money and physical resources will need to be devoted to security efforts.

Wind and Steel

One of the world's leading experts on wind energy is Stanford engineering professor Mark Jacobson. He's a staunch believer in wind's potential to provide the world with virtually endless—and green—energy that can turn on our lights, power our factories, and even fill our gas tanks.

According to Jacobson and his colleague Cristina Archer, globally wind could provide around 72 terawatts of energy. This is equivalent to around 54 billion tons of oil, or more than five times as much energy as the world currently uses a year. In 2007, for instance, the world's total energy consumption, including oil, nuclear, coal, and everything else, came to the equivalent of around 10 billion tons of oil.

In other words, theoretically, wind could do it all. In fact, if we could harness just 20 percent of the wind that blows, the world could free itself from its dependence on all other forms of energy, according to Jacobson's studies.

Jacobson presented his case for wind in two articles published in *Science*, the first in 2001 and the second about four years later. In the first, he argued that when all costs are factored in, wind is the cheapest way of generating electricity—even cheaper than coal. To be fair, in calculating the cost of coal, Jacobson added on direct health-care costs to society stemming from coal's role as a lung irritant. He did not, however, include any costs stemming from greenhouse gas emissions. The second article went even further. It argued that wind energy is cheap enough to be used to create fuel for automobiles.

Specifically, Jacobson wrote that wind-generated hydrolysis—that is, using wind to generate electricity to separate a hydrogen atom from the water molecule H_2O—would be a cheaper way to fuel automobiles than refining gasoline from oil. This unequivocal and provocative assertion was backed up with a tremendous amount of detailed analysis that to the best of our knowledge has not been seriously challenged. Jacobson seemed to be offering a clear road to a hydrogen economy in which wind would serve as a cost-effective means of getting the hydrogen. Fueling automobiles with hydrogen-based fuel cells has long been a dream of alternative energy advocates, and Jacobson seemed to have found the way.

How realistic is this vision, and how much might it cost? In a recent conversation with us, Jacobson estimated the United States would need around 700,000 wind turbines to satisfy all its energy needs. He estimated the initial costs to be around $3 trillion, including the costs of constructing the turbines along with other essential costs such as setting up transmission wires to the grid. But once the turbines were in place, the costs of generating electricity would be minimal. Turbines have life spans of twenty years or longer. In saying that wind is cheaper than coal or other competing methods of generating electricity, Jacobson was saying that if you spread out the initial construction costs over twenty years, you'd spend less than if you obtained electricity from coal or other sources. According to Jacobson, the savings from wind would be so great than the initial costs would be recovered in around ten years or so.

Jacobson is an exceptionally bright researcher who knows the technology of wind energy inside and out. But we think that in projecting the costs of wind energy and hence its potential to take over as the energy of the future, he's missed something critical: the rising costs of the raw materials needed to construct wind turbines, in particular the iron ore that goes into making steel. This important oversight is an excellent illustration of the tunnel vision among scientists we discussed in the preceding chapter and of why it's so important to bring specialists from different areas together.

In 2008, wind energy will account for about 1 percent of America's electricity needs. This is up dramatically from just a few years ago, when wind made almost no contribution. Typically, when a new technology comes on board, you expect to see a "learning curve effect"—that is, you look for costs to come down over time as those producing the technology perfect the process. The transistor is a prime example: as it has matured as a product, its cost has decreased, literally, many millionfold. Not many products will come down to that extent, but still, prices should almost always come down.

And this was true with wind technology—until recently. Advances in turbine technology brought down some basic costs in constructing wind farms. Yet despite these advances, Jacobson acknowledged that the costs of wind turbines had risen about 20 percent over the past several years.

The reason is that the learning curve savings have been more than offset by the rising costs of raw materials. In 2008, one of the world's major iron ore companies managed to negotiate a nearly 100 percent increase in iron ore, a basic ingredient in making steel, which in turn is a basic component of wind turbines. *Steeply rising prices and growing shortages of iron ore make it unlikely that the United States ever could rely on wind power as a central source of electricity.*

It's not just that the costs have risen already. The real dilemma is that if we proceeded to multiply the number of wind turbines by a hundred times—to go from 1 percent to 100 percent of our electricity—it would enormously increase the demand for steel. In fact, it's possible there would not be enough iron ore available in the world to accommodate these needs, at any price. And this accounts just for converting the United States to wind energy. If the rest of the world tried to follow suit, there's almost no doubt it would be impossible.

Once again it comes back to the vicious circles we described in chapter 2. As oil becomes scarcer and more expensive, it becomes more expensive to find other raw materials, including iron ore. And actually, the relationships are so entangled that it's not even clear what is cause and what is effect. That is, to explain the high and rising price of oil, you could plausibly argue that the scarcity of iron ore, which is needed for drilling equipment, is the culprit, rather than vice versa. It really doesn't matter—the point is that there's no way to treat all these commodities separately.

CHAPTER 9

More on Alternative Energies

Solar Energy

While wind theoretically could meet all our energy needs five times over, that pales in comparison to what we could reap from the sun. Enough energy from the sun hits the Earth in a single *hour* to supply the world with all the energy it now uses in an entire year. No wonder solar energy is often viewed as the ultimate way out of our oil dependency. If we could harness the sun's energy in a resource-efficient manner that produced a net energy gain, we would have a truly limitless supply of energy forever. Those, however, are significant ifs.

Worldwide, solar energy has been growing by leaps and bounds, but it still accounts for far less than 1 percent of global energy consumption. The reason it hasn't made bigger inroads is its cost. And the reason this virtually infinite source of energy costs so much has everything to do with the vicious circles among natural resources.

So far, two chief ways of capturing solar energy have been developed and are in use: solar cells, made from photovoltaic materials, and solar collectors. Of the two approaches, solar cells, which convert sunlight directly into electricity, have caught on more and offer the greater potential. Solar cell technology is still evolving, and the hope is that breakthroughs will occur that will make solar cells cheaper and more efficient, leading to wider use.

Most solar cells in operation today use silicon, which is more efficient than other materials that have been developed, meaning it converts a higher proportion of the sunlight that strikes it into usable energy. But silicon has drawbacks. It's a difficult substance to work with, requiring a lot of skill and effort to be produced in a form suitable for use in solar cells. In addition, its manufacturing process requires large amounts of both water and energy.

A newer alternative to silicon is thin film photovoltaics. Though thin film is less efficient than silicon, and thus it takes more of it to generate the same amount of electricity, it's nonetheless cheaper because far fewer resources go into making it in the first place. And ongoing research will probably produce technological improvements in thin film that will increase its efficiency, further bringing down the costs of the electricity it generates.

Still, when you ask the key question—do solar cells produce a net gain in energy—the answer isn't clear, either for the present or looking ahead. Right now, the direct energy consumed in the manufacturing of solar cells is somewhat less than the amount of energy they generate, so there would seem to be a net energy gain. But you have to consider other factors, too, before making a final determination.

One such issue is storage. Since the sun shines only during the day, and not all the time during the day, it's essential to find ways to store solar energy if we're to rely on it completely. (Wind energy presents a similar problem, of course, since wind doesn't blow all the time, but the problem is more easily dealt with. Jacobson's estimate of 700,000 wind turbines, for example, builds in enough redundancy to deal with the problem of intermittency.) *To date, there simply is no economical way to store solar energy.* Both compressed air and battery storage, the two methods developed so far, are very expensive. And to calculate whether solar cells truly result in a net energy gain, you need to factor in the energy that goes into constructing storage systems. For definitive answers, more research is needed. In any case, there will be geographical differences in solar cells' effectiveness—they will, of course, be more energy efficient in sunnier locations.

For now, one thing we do know, and the reason solar cells aren't in wider use, is that once you take into account installation and maintenance costs, electricity from solar cells and especially those that use silicon is considerably more expensive than other sources of electricity. Since costs mainly reflect material and energy inputs, this suggests that solar cells consume more resources, including energy, than other ways of generating electricity.

One other problem applies especially to thin film photovoltaics. The most successful thin film technology is cadmium telluride, which has been pioneered by the company First Solar (whose stock consequently has soared over the past several years). The goal of First Solar, a company that has made it a habit to exceed expectations, is for this technology to reach "grid parity" within a few years. In other words, the hope is that continuing improvements will soon mean that thin film cells will be able to supply electricity to the grid more economically than coal- or gas-fired plants can do.

That would be a major step forward. Unfortunately, there's a catch. Thin film technology relies on tellurium, one of the world's rarest metals and one that also is needed in memory chips, optical discs, and as a strengthener in lead and copper. Between 2000 and 2006, tellurium prices climbed more than sevenfold, outpacing almost all other commodities. Right now, tellurium-based solar cells provide a tiny fraction of 1 percent of the world's energy needs, and thus demand for the metal from the solar cell industry has negligible impact on its cost. As soon as you tried to scale this technology up in a significant way, though, demand for tellurium would soar. Some geologists believe that even under existing uses, tellurium will be in very short supply by 2020. Clearly, any attempt to rapidly ramp up production of First Solar's thin film solar cells would bring shortages on far sooner.

And it gets even more complicated, as vicious circles among commodities once again make life tough. Most tellurium comes from the refining of copper. But as energy costs rise, mining for copper will become ever more expensive, which in turn will put even more pressure on tellurium prices.

In sum, while photovoltaics certainly may have a role to play, using them on a large scale is far less of a sure thing. At the very least, the technologies for thin film itself and for solar energy storage will need to improve. Moreover, as oil and other traditional energy sources become scarcer, it will become trickier than ever to measure whether solar cells produce a net energy gain. That's because even if it is energy positive to use solar cells today, the parameters will shift if they start being produced in far higher numbers and energy scarcity becomes much more sensitive to marginal uses—that is, as energy gets scarcer, any additional use has a greater proportional effect on the amount that's left.

Solar collectors are the other approach to capturing the sun's energy. They concentrate the heat of the sun and use it to boil water, which then generates electricity. Like photovoltaics, solar collectors can only work directly when the sun is out and thus require some means of storage. Moreover, the materials used to make the collectors include a variety of resources, such as aluminum and copper, whose price and scarcity would be dramatically affected if collectors were put into widespread use.

Because of their high costs, collectors are not a good way to generate electricity. Though the technology no doubt will improve, it's likely that—as we discussed in the previous chapter with wind turbines—the gains from this learning curve will be at least partially offset by the growing scarcity of the metals needed to construct the collectors.

Geothermal Energy

Geothermal energy is, literally, energy from the earth. Throughout the globe, heat is continually produced in a layer below the Earth's crust. This heat can be tapped to bring water to high temperatures, and the resulting steam can power large plants and produce electricity. Theoretically, the amount of geothermal energy available is essentially limitless. But it's easily accessible in only a few parts of the world, and if we tried to expand its use to other areas on a large scale, we'd once again bump into resource limits.

In places with volcanic activity, such as Iceland—a country that by some estimates gets 50 percent of its energy from geothermal sources—geothermal energy is easier to access because it is so close to the surface. Elsewhere, though, reaching it requires drilling holes deep into the earth. This carries risks—it can lead to instability in the land—and entails injecting large amounts of water, some of which escapes with contaminants. Beyond its need for water, geothermal energy also uses significant amounts of metals needed for the drills and other equipment required to transmit geothermal heat into electricity.

Still, we think that in any calculus of costs and benefits, geothermal energy could well come out ahead of nuclear energy. While water scarcities are an issue for both these energies, geothermal energy doesn't depend upon a whole separate energy source, the way nuclear energy relies upon uranium as a feedstock. And, of course, with geothermal you avoid all the headaches and costs related to storing radioactive by-products and dealing with security issues.

Before geothermal energy can contribute significantly, though, a lot more research is needed to figure out how to best develop geothermal resources. The most definitive study on geothermal energy was done at MIT in late 2006. Estimating that fifteen years of research will be needed to develop the proper techniques, the study concludes that by midcentury this energy source could provide a significant portion of U.S. electricity needs. Unfortunately, though, we probably don't have forty years to wait.

Biofuels and Biomass

Today, every time you pump gasoline into your car's tank, you're almost surely putting in some corn-based ethanol—a type of biofuel—along with petroleum products. That's because early this decade the United States began requiring that ethanol be mixed with gasoline in an effort to reduce our dependence on foreign oil. Indeed, biofuels have been the cornerstone so far of the country's alternative energy efforts. But while they may have some long-term potential as an alternative energy, they also present a lot of negatives and troubling trade-offs, and we think it was a terrible place to start.

Ethanol produced from corn involves trade-offs among land, water, food, and energy. The most obvious conflict is between food and energy. Prior to the new regulations, corn in the United States had spent a generation or so trading at around $2 a bushel (see chart on page 106). When demand for corn surged because of its new role as a fuel, farmers gladly planted massive amounts of the vegetable at the expense of other crops. And, surprise, surprise, other agricultural products, such as soybeans, surged in price.

The problem is that there simply isn't enough land available to accommodate ethanol from corn, corn for food for both humans and cattle, and other agricultural products. As the chart shows, corn prices surged well past previous records. And these prior spikes

Corn Prices

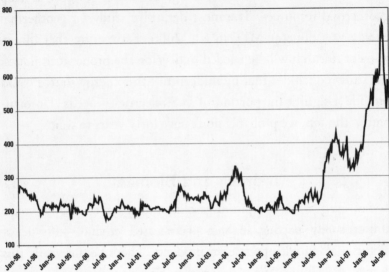

Source: Bloomberg

came during periods of severe drought. The current surge has stemmed not from ephemeral events but from a systemic change.

Ethanol has other drawbacks as well. It requires a lot of water, first to grow the corn and then in processing the corn into usable fuel. Besides water, it also depends on several other critical natural resources as well, including natural gas, potash, and phosphorous, all three of which are used to make fertilizers. Because all these resources are finite, ethanol can't be relied upon over the long term as an energy source. Some experts, in fact, believe we could run out of phosphorous within the next twenty years, which could be devastating for world food production. The emphasis on ethanol has contributed to steep rises in fertilizer prices, which have climbed considerably faster during this decade than even oil and most other commodities. Potash, a necessary ingredient in most fertilizers, has surged more than fourfold in under four years, as the next chart shows.

Potash

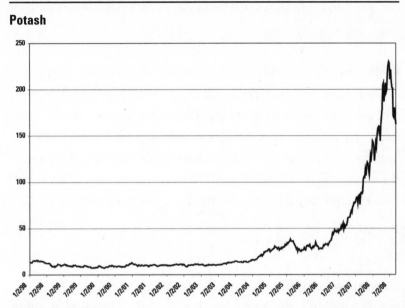

Source: Bloomberg

Of course, ethanol isn't the only reason food and fertilizer prices have been surging. The growing demand in developing nations for more food and in particular for more protein-rich food is the most basic factor of all. We live in a world in which about 2 billion people are surviving on less than $2 a day. Continued economic development will mean this massive population living near starvation will be moving up the food chain. For the United States to emphasize corn-based ethanol as a fuel pits our need for energy squarely against the world's need for food. An article in *Foreign Affairs* argues that meeting the ethanol target would consume as much as half the nation's corn production, driving corn prices even higher (C. Ford Runge and Benjamin Senauer, "How Biofuels Could Starve the Poor," May/June 2007) and leaving less land to grow food.

Beyond this moral issue, though, it isn't even clear that ethanol is effective in reducing our need for oil. Many scientific studies have concluded that producing ethanol from corn consumes more energy than it can provide. The same goes for ethanol or biodiesel made from most other types of plant material (ibid.). If this is really the case, the government's current plan to boost ethanol use fivefold by 2017 will likely only increase our need for foreign oil.

Moreover, some studies show that contrary to popular belief, ethanol is not even a green energy. The manufacturing process emits many particulates and is strongly associated with asthma and other lung diseases, not all that different from coal. To accurately compute the overall costs of ethanol, you'd have to add health costs, which could become considerable if ethanol became more broadly used.

Cars

Cars and other vehicles account for around 70 percent of U.S. oil use. If we didn't have to devote so much oil to gasoline, it might extend considerably the amount of time we have before we get to Absolute Peak Oil. In any case, at some point in the fairly near future it will become essential to find other fuels for cars as oil grows increasingly expensive and ultimately barely available.

Of the various alternatives to oil we've discussed, only biofuels can be used directly in car engines, and as we've seen, they are probably a terrible way to go. Other energy sources, though, can power cars indirectly by creating electricity that can be introduced into cars in various forms to replace gasoline.

In the previous chapter, for instance, we referred to Mark Jacobson's study of wind electrolysis. In this process, energy from wind is used to generate electricity, which is then applied to water molecules so as to split off hydrogen. The resulting pure hydrogen is an energy carrier. One way to use it is to store it in fuel cells and use it in cars to replace gasoline.

Jacobson has argued that after taking all direct and indirect costs into account, the process is actually cheaper than refining gasoline from oil. As we noted, though, his analysis wasn't dynamic. It didn't consider the rising costs over time of building wind turbines or the rising costs of the infrastructure for transporting and storing the hydrogen. It also ignored the costs associated with platinum, an essential component of fuel cells. The small numbers of cars equipped to run on hydrogen fuel cells that have been produced have made it easy to avoid facing up to the major limitation imposed by platinum shortages. *But if we tried to have a meaningful number of the world's vehicles—say, 150 million—run on fuel cells, we simply wouldn't have enough of the metal.* In sum, we're not convinced that hydrogen fuel cells will ever be a competitive source of power for cars.

Interest has been growing in two other possibilities: cars that run on batteries (including hybrid cars that use both batteries and gasoline) and cars that run on natural gas. As we've noted, natural gas cars are now being championed in a big way by T. Boone Pickens, while in some parts of the United States the huge disparities in price between natural gas and gasoline have caused demand for natural gas cars to surge. One result of the attention being paid to these efforts is that it seems to be fostering a sense that we can deal with worsening oil shortages anytime simply by ramping up production of these types of vehicles. At the very least, these would seem like virtuous causes to support.

You won't be surprised to learn it's not that simple. For many reasons, cars that run on fuels other than gasoline aren't likely to be the answer to oil shortages. Perhaps the biggest reason is that we simply won't be able to switch to them quickly enough on a large enough scale.

One big obstacle is the hundreds of millions of gasoline-run cars that are in existence already. *Automotive Digest* estimates that by 2010 the world's total vehicle population will top 730 million. Every year, around 50 million new cars are sold, or around 8 percent of the total vehicle population. *So even if all the world's carmakers were able to completely retool and within a year offer only cars powered by something other than gasoline, you'd be replacing less than 10 percent of the total vehicle fleet.* Meanwhile, there still would be nearly 700 million older vehicles cruising around guzzling gasoline.

In other words, whenever new types of cars are discussed, the reference point typically is how many of them are sold in a year. But the much more relevant reference point is the total vehicle population.

Regardless, there is zero chance that automakers really could completely retool so that going forward all new cars would run on something other than gasoline. Look at Toyota's hybrid Prius, for instance. Sales have been growing at a torrid rate, and demand for these vehicles is booming in the United States and elsewhere. *But hybrids still represent little more than 2 percent of U.S. car sales.* Thus, in a year, hybrids replace a virtually meaningless percentage of the U.S. car fleet.

Hybrid cars are generally viewed as just the first stop on the way to cars that are completely independent of gasoline. Battery-powered cars and plug-in hybrids—which use electricity from the grid for most of their power—are often considered the cars of the future. But battery-based cars have their own set of problems, and these problems loom larger once you start thinking about replacing the entire population of cars.

General Motors is coming out with a battery-operated car that it has dubbed the Volt. It is powered by the latest in battery technology: lithium-based batteries. But lithium isn't a renewable resource. It's also not clear that various problems associated with lithium have been resolved; for instance, it's highly reactive and prone to explosions.

Equally telling is the relatively small number of these cars in the offing. According to the May-June 2008 issue of *Technology Review*, General Motors at best plans to produce a few hundred thousand of the vehicles within the first several years. That's not even a rounding error in terms of overall vehicle population.

Finally, let's look more closely at the potential in cars powered by natural gas. And once again, the situation becomes radically different once it's a question of scaling up the numbers of cars in a big way.

First, natural gas is a finite resource. And despite some impressive discoveries of gas in the United States, production has been increasing by only a few percent a year, barely enough to satisfy growing demand for electricity.

Moreover, unlike oil, natural gas fields are exhausted very quickly. Oil wells can often continue producing for more than a half century. *But natural gas finds tend to get depleted very rapidly.* It is unlikely that there is anywhere near enough natural gas to sustain a meaningful number of automobiles in the United States for an extended period of time.

Pickens has tried to deal with this objection by pointing out that if we used wind to replace natural gas as a source of electricity, all the gas now going into electricity generation would become available for cars. That could give natural gas cars a longer lease on life. But we'd still eventually run into limits imposed by finite supplies of natural gas. And meanwhile, as with cars powered by electricity, automakers would have to retool in order to turn out natural gas–powered cars, and we'd have to create a huge continent-wide infrastructure to make sure we have enough natural gas filling stations to service all the cars. And we'd have to be willing to do all this even though the number of natural gas–powered vehicles that we would be adding each year would be an insignificant portion of total vehicles on the road—all the while knowing that eventually we'd be running into the same kinds of shortages and rising costs with natural gas that we're facing now with oil.

The largest maker of natural gas cars is Honda. As of February 2008, its natural gas–powered Civic was sold out until at least midyear. But despite very strong demand, *Honda plans to increase production from a measly 1,000 a year to a measly 2,000 a year.* Retooling these autos isn't just a question of a couple of tweaks in engine design. A natural gas engine, which fits in the back of the car, is much larger than a gasoline engine. It would take massive capital investments to produce a meaningful number of such vehicles. And unlike most capital investments, which are intended to result in products with long life spans, in this case the dilemma is that the more popular natural gas vehicles become, and the greater the numbers of them that go on the road, the sooner natural gas will become in permanently short supply.

There is also a real question as to whether natural gas will produce a net energy gain as we are forced to seek it in places that present greater challenges. Matthew Simmons, for example, whom we cited in chapter 1, argues that it probably won't. That's because the recent surge in production has come primarily from shale formations, and drilling into shale, he says, involves higher costs and more energy inputs than drilling vertically into deposits in the ground or the ocean. Thus, Simmons argues that future efforts to obtain natural gas will use up more energy than they obtain, making the sharply increased reserves and production we've recently seen something of a chimera.

In sum, with cars as with everything else relating to alternative energies, all the key questions revolve around whether we have enough resources to make any particular approach sustainable when we attempt to apply it on a large scale over time. If not, *pursuing avenues with only short-term potential could simply make the situation worse*, as we commit large amounts of scarce resources—those that go into the cars themselves and those that go into the infrastructure needed to support them—to something that eventually will be a dead end.

CHAPTER 10

Buying Time

A bsolute Peaks and Game Over are lurking somewhere over
the horizon, inching ever closer. The only way to dispel their
malignant presence is to develop and implement alternative energies on a large enough scale to break our dependence on oil—and
to do so before we run out of time. As the preceding chapters show,
though, this won't be easy, because a lot of factors and trade-offs
must be weighed to ensure we make intelligent choices. And it
won't just spontaneously happen as we get close to zero hour. We
need to commit well before then to a national program of research
and implementation. This won't happen overnight. Meanwhile,
growing scarcities and rising prices of energy and other commodities will make the job even harder, while contributing to rising
economic turbulence that will add further to the difficulty.

It's logical to think that anything we can do to buy time in
which to accomplish the critical job of making the transition to
alternative energies would be well worth doing. If we can extend
the number of years we have before reaching Absolute Peak Oil and
Absolute Peak Commodities by husbanding our resources, or by
finding new supplies of oil and other commodities, we'd potentially

have that much more of a chance of being successful in our quest. We could carefully structure the enormous research effort that is needed, recruit the best people, and figure out the best incentives to get private industry involved in the most constructive way.

Buying time might indeed be a worthwhile effort, but it's not as simple as is often thought. An obvious place to start might seem to be to cut demand for oil by conservation, which could be achieved through various stratagems, anything from switching to fluorescent lights to driving more fuel-efficient cars to driving less, period. But as we'll show, *the jury is out on just how much use conservation might be*. It might buy us time, but it's likely to be less effective than many of the numbers often cited indicate, and it might not help at all.

The other approach focuses on the supply side, looking for ways to extract more oil and other essential commodities and to do so at lower costs, expending fewer resources in the process. One possibility along these lines might be to try to pare away some of the complexities that currently burden and inhibit exploration and development. If this could be achieved, oil companies and other natural resource companies might find their costs of doing business coming down, making it feasible to move ahead more quickly with more projects. There is no clear path, though, to reducing complexities, nor is it clear whether it can be done quickly enough to bring costs down in time. And there's a good chance that if anyone really started to tackle the issue of complexities—trying to simplify taxes or reduce environmental constraints, to name just two possibilities that come to mind—it might prove only a distraction.

A potentially more rewarding avenue to boosting supplies, thereby buying time, would be to apply some innovative mathematical techniques to the way that geology is carried out. We look at these techniques later in this chapter.

Of course, the big question is whether, given humanity's track record, there's any hope that we'll use any time we gain wisely. Will we say, "Oh, boy, look, we've just found more oil and watched prices drop, so let's put lots of money now into developing alternative energies"? Or will we fall back into complacency, as we did after the oil crises in the last century?

It's certainly an open question. Meanwhile, in the sincere hope that we've learned from the past, let's look at some potential ways we might buy time and push the onset of Absolute Peak Oil and Absolute Peak Commodities further down the road.

A Dog Chasing Its Tail

Many people instinctively want to address the problem of our dependency on oil by finding ways to use less of it. Congress's Joint Economic Committee, for instance, recently conducted a hearing titled "Efficiency: The Hidden Secret to Solving Our Energy Crisis." As reported glowingly in "The Winning Hand" (August 5, 2008) by *New York Times* columnist Bob Herbert, it put the spotlight on the gamut of ways to cut down on energy consumption, from buildings with more efficient heating and cooling systems to cars with high mileage ratings to energy-efficient lightbulbs. Herbert quotes Dan Reicher, a former assistant secretary at the Department of Energy, as saying: "From cars and homes to factories and offices, we know how to cost-effectively deliver vast quantities of energy savings today."

Conservation understandably seems to most people like a no-brainer. At the very least, how could it hurt to use oil and other resources more frugally? But one of the most fundamental points in this book is that in our complex world, and particularly when it comes to commodities, everything is connected to everything else. And this is as true of conservation as it is about anything else we've touched on.

Let's start with a simple, oft-suggested (though politically unpalatable) form of conservation: taxing gasoline so that motorists will drive less. Suppose the tax does what it's supposed to do, and gasoline consumption goes down as consumers turn to more fuel-efficient cars or find ways to drive less. You would assume that conservation has been victorious, and that we've struck a blow against our dependency on oil.

It's not that simple. Because we're using less gasoline and hence less oil, oil prices will be lower than if we had not instituted the gasoline tax. And that means that it's likely that more oil will be consumed for other purposes. People might be more willing to keep their thermostats set high in winter, for instance, if they're paying less for the extra heat.

Incidentally, this works in reverse, too. It's easy to criticize politicians who, in the midst of a political campaign, suggest such steps as a tax holiday on gas to help out the struggling consumer. After all, lowered taxes would only encourage consumers to drive more, consuming more oil—surely the last thing we should want to foster in an oil-constrained world. But while we're not saying we favor such proposals—and we certainly don't think they stem from pure economic analysis on the part of said politicians—it's still true that the same logic as applied above would tell us that more gasoline consumption would boost oil prices overall, leading to efforts to conserve.

The bottom line is that specific conservation taxes amount to the proverbial dog chasing its tail. They're not an effective approach.

But what about a uniform tax on all carbon-based energy—would that get around the problem? No, and for a similar reason writ large. Remember, the United States and the rest of the developed world are part of a global community, and we're far outnumbered—six to one—by the developing world. And the developing world can't develop without continuing to increase its consumption of oil and other natural resources. Through taxes on carbon-based energy, the U.S. no doubt could sharply curtail its own oil consumption. But by driving prices lower, this would merely mean that oil will become cheaper than it otherwise would have been, which in turn would simply encourage its greater use by the developing world.

This doesn't mean that conservation wouldn't have some welcome short-term effects. It might, for instance, make the dollar stronger, which, assuming that oil continues to be priced in dollars, would bring down oil prices for the United States and make oil somewhat more expensive in the developing world. In the end, though, the dollar isn't likely to strengthen for long, because we're unlikely to be able to conserve enough to reduce our consumption of foreign oil in a big way.

Conservation could, possibly, buy us some time. But we don't think it will buy nearly as much as its strongest advocates believe. To put the focus on conservation, in our opinion, would be diverting attention away from other steps we should be taking.

Data, Data, Everywhere

We have long been distressed by the modern world's obsession with processing data at ever faster rates, as if speed itself is the ultimate goal. In our view, this emphasis is senseless, and indeed, over the past few decades, technological advances haven't been in areas that are of much use. We first wrote about this nine years ago in our book *Defying the Market*. Written during the height of the technology bubble, when information technology was widely viewed as offering solutions to any and all problems, the book discussed all the ways in which "faster is better" wasn't coming up with solutions to real-world problems.

The focus on ever faster calculating speed has continued, however. Recent technological innovations continue to focus mainly on increasing the number of calculations per second that computers can perform and on helping us disseminate information faster. And the more data we can handle, the more we try to handle. The more calculations computers can perform, the more functions we invent for them to carry out. The more data computers can store and transmit easily, the more data we create and save—and the more that Internet traffic rises. Rather than reduce complexity, our technologies add to it. And much of the data generated and disseminated is trivial.

Thomas Watson, IBM's chairman in the 1940s, is famous for having said, "I think there is a world market for maybe five computers." He saw computers simply as tools to be used in a handful of scientific research laboratories, where the time needed for mathematical calculations was a serious impediment. No one of his era could have imagined using computers to exchange jokes, swap recipes, or meet your future mate.

We could give lots of examples of areas where faster calculating speed hasn't led to worthwhile results. It's striking, for instance, that most innovative drugs developed in recent years haven't resulted from computers' ability to analyze the human genome. Rather, they have been found in nature or else have resulted from brilliant human insights.

In another area, today computers play a major role on Wall Street, and Wall Street has embraced computerized trading on the grounds that computers can transmit and respond to information a lot faster than human beings can. Software that executes trades on its own (with human guidance) now accounts for around one-third of stock trades in the United States. By 2010 it is expected to be responsible for half of all trades. A financial arms race is taking place as companies hurry to develop software that can get the upper hand on other computers making trades and spot disparities among markets.

But while you might assume that information technology would add stability to the financial system, since computers are dispassionate traders, this hasn't been true at several critical junctures. The market crash of 1987 was one example. The failure of Long-Term Capital Management in 1998 was another. That massive debacle was brought on largely because of the inadequacy, once circumstances went awry, of complex computer models. The recent subprime debacle is another example of a crisis that could not have occurred without all the complexity made possible by computers and that wasn't averted by the ability of computers to process data.

So why are we going into this here? Our point is that we need to start applying our technologies where they're really needed—in particular in trying to deal with resource shortages—and to stop looking at data and at faster processing speed as mere ends in themselves. *Data isn't the same as information—and it's not the same as wisdom. Fast isn't better: smarter is better.*

Geology in the Dark Ages

Luckily, there are some rays of hope. We referred above to innovative mathematical techniques that we think have great potential in bringing geology into the twenty-first century. If so, it would be none too soon, for geology, which is so essential to helping us buy time by finding more oil and other resources, has been languishing in the dark ages.

This was brought home to me in a personal way about a year ago, when I was privileged to sit next to one of the world's finest geologists. One of his achievements had been to discover one of the world's largest silver deposits. These days, mineral exploration generally relies on mounds of geologic data, including electromagnetic, chemical, seismic, and gravitational test results. But none of this data aided this particular discovery.

Rather, the geologist began his search by remembering a letter he had received nearly twenty years earlier and had filed away in a steel filing cabinet. It was from an investor who had suggested that the geologist explore a particular area where silver was said to literally glisten on the ground. Now, twenty years later, the geologist decided to visit the area. He did not see any silver, but using his intuition, he selected a place to begin exploratory drilling. The samples confirmed the existence of an exceptionally rich silver deposit.

Two aspects of this story are notable. First, it points out the value of human intuition, when coupled with training and experience. Although the spot did not seem promising at first, the geologist didn't walk away. Rather, he used his instincts to select a location that turned out to be a winner.

And second, it illustrates how badly we need to find better, more reliable ways to locate promising exploration targets. We have amassed huge amounts of data about every accessible part of the planet, much of which is catalogued in computers. Yet geologists lack the tools to analyze that data effectively and zero in on the most likely exploration sites. Instead, they have to rely heavily on intuition.

As a result, today the normal success rate in drilling for minerals can be up to one in several hundred. For oil companies, the rate is no better than one in three. That means a lot of resources get squandered in wasted drilling and exploring, and it adds to the costs shouldered by resource companies. Anything that could improve geological productivity would be enormously helpful in buying time and ensuring that the resources we have are put to effective use.

Hope in New Math

Math has been developed over the past several years that could play a big role in improving the productivity of geologic exploration. The leader in creating this new math is Yale professor Ronald Coifman. Coifman, a winner of the National Medal of Science as well as of a Sustained Excellence Award from the Department of Defense's research arm, DARPA, heads what is arguably the most forward-thinking research group in the world. Recognized as one of the world's great theoretical mathematicians, he has managed to apply the most abstract mathematics to devising exactly the kinds of real-world applications needed. His work could go far in bringing geology into the modern age.

Coifman has invented a whole new toolbox that turns raw data into usable information in ways that can't be done using standard mathematical techniques. For an idea of what this means, consider the task of organizing books in a library. The traditional approach would be to arrange the books by subject matter and author. Coifman's work, however, offers another possibility: arranging books by their actual content, surmised by looking at the raw "data" embedded in books—the words they contain.

To collect this raw data, we'd start by taking each book in the library and counting the number of times each word appears in the books. Then, two books at a time, we'd compare their lists of word counts, after which we'd assign each pair a number that is proportional to how many words they have in common. We can think of this as a crude measure of affinity; the more words they share, the greater the affinity.

Now suppose you're at your local library reading Charles Dickens's *Hard Times* and you'd like to find a similar book. You look at the list of books that have a high number of words in common with *Hard Times* and select one at random. It turns out to be *David Copperfield*. No surprise: both books are by the same author, so it seems plausible they would use many of the same words. Then you look at the list of books with a high affinity to *David Copperfield* and again pick one at random. You keep repeating the process. At the end of the day, the final book you've picked is *A Christmas Carol*.

The next day you come back to the same library and, again starting with *Hard Times*, repeat the process. But while you go through the same number of books as on the previous day, you won't necessarily end up with *A Christmas Carol*. Remember, each new book you pick up is chosen at random from a list of books with high affinities to *Hard Times*, so you'll find different books each time. On this second day, for instance, the last book in the chain might be *Vanity Fair*, by William Thackeray, a Dickens contemporary. On the third day, once again starting with *Hard Times*, you might end with Upton Sinclair's *The Jungle*—not Dickens or a Dickens contemporary but an author who, like Dickens, wrote about social injustice.

After many days you look at all the books that were your final picks. Some are by Dickens, some by authors from the same period as Dickens, and some by authors who covered the same themes as Dickens.

But here's the intriguing thing: it turns out that many of the books on the list don't share many words with *Hard Times*. They do, however, share words with books that share words with books that share words with books—and so on—that share words with *Hard Times*. And this was enough to uncover books that are related to *Hard Times* in certain significant ways.

The next step is to repeat the entire process with each and every book the library contains. This makes it possible to replace the original affinities between books based on word counts with a more sophisticated measure of affinity derived from looking at which book we'll likely end up with when we start with any given book. These new affinities take the process a giant step forward. They organize the library according to the content of its books rather than by the words they have in common, and they make it easy for readers who like a particular book to find others that they're also likely to enjoy.

The upshot: we have taken some basic data about books—their word frequencies—and turned it into useful information that can organize an entire library in a revolutionary way that is potentially highly rewarding to readers seeking books they would enjoy reading.

Of course, we're not particularly disposed to use such an approach in libraries—we are just trying to offer a simple illustration. With a library, you probably would do as well or better simply consulting the librarian, who is likely to know literature inside and out and would be more than happy to talk to you and help you find books you would enjoy. The point, in fact, is that when it comes to books, the information about what they contain is already known.

Coifman's techniques come into their own when applied in fields where there is no such top-down knowledge in prior existence. In these areas, his techniques work to uncover meaningful relationships by organizing data in original ways. And indeed, Coifman's mathematical techniques have been fruitfully applied in many diverse areas, from speech recognition to image processing.

We think they could make a major contribution as well in an area where they have yet to be applied: geology. Instead of comparing word counts in books, the idea would be to organize data about oil wells and mines, comparing traits of the wells and mines that have succeeded with those of the wells and mines that have failed. The goal would be to pinpoint likely locations for new wells and mines. The potential for helping oil and natural resource companies find productive wells and mines far more efficiently than they now do, wasting far fewer resources in the process, is enormous. It could make a big difference in how much time we have before reaching Absolute Peak Oil and Absolute Peak Commodities and Game Over.

CHAPTER 11

Denial and Disaster

What are the chances we will act in time? What will it take to get us to act? How bad will things need to get? And if we wait for them to get that bad, will there be enough time left?

As we discussed in the preceding chapter, buying more time by conserving or by squeezing out additional supplies of oil and other resources won't mean much unless we use that extra time wisely. Complacency is the enemy. And complacency is a strong force, because it stems from an even stronger facet of human nature, the capacity for denial, which on an individual level can be necessary for self-preservation.

Human beings hate change and have trouble adjusting to abrupt changes. Thus, we'd rather put off making changes for as long as possible, which we justify by clinging to the belief that maybe change won't be necessary after all. Usually, of course, it would be far easier in the long run to make needed changes sooner rather than later. But that's logic, not human nature.

Unfortunately, this may mean that it may take a major disaster to finally break through our wall of denial concerning the severity of resource shortages. *At that point, when finally forced to act, we will start making heroic efforts to fix our problems.* But the more time that has elapsed before we get to that point, the higher the costs will be and the worse the prognosis for success.

If, having read the preceding chapters, you've been convinced by what we've said so far, you have to be concerned by these questions. We certainly are. The problems we've identified are real, and the general nature of the solution is clear. It's frustrating to think that we'll continue to waste precious time without doing anything, or enough. Let's look at what we're up against in terms of innate human tendencies.

Resistance to Change

The great French sociologist Emile Durkheim studied the pain that people feel when the circumstances of their lives undergo sudden changes. One of his insights was that such abrupt changes could be psychologically painful even if on the surface they would appear to be for the better. In his classic work *Suicide*, first published in 1897, Durkheim observed that sudden changes in one's economic status, whether they involve having much more money or much less, typically provoke higher rates of suicide (and therefore, by implication, misery). Durkheim explained this by postulating that society helps people find contentment in life by setting appropriate boundaries for both their aspirations and their failures. When the boundaries are suddenly changed, individuals lose their bearings. They feel disconnected from society and from their peers, and as a result are overwhelmed by feelings of discomfort and discontent.

Abrupt change, in other words, causes stress. Winning a fortune in a lottery might sound like a dream come true, but many lottery winners end up less happy than before as they worry that others envy them and are only after their money. At the same time, bad events, such as losing a job or having your business fail, also cause tremendous stress, bringing on feelings of failure and shame on top of the economic loss.

The message is that for change to be tolerable, it is better if the entire society can change together in a gradual, coordinated, and voluntary way that preserves the social order. Change that disrupts the social order, that breaks the rules favoring or disfavoring certain groups or activities, often leads to widespread distress.

Unfortunately, in our current economic situation, the time to make gradual, tolerable changes in response to resource shortages has come and gone. This means that society is in for a high level of dislocation and misery. A reluctance to believe this, however, is keeping denial alive and widespread.

An Early Warning

The fate of one famous earlier warning about resource shortages is instructive. In 1972, the Club of Rome published a controversial but important report called *The Limits to Growth*. In effect, it used a mathematical model to project an eventual worldwide catastrophe resulting from natural resource depletion. It reads in part:

> If the present growth trends in world population, industrialization, pollution, food production, and resource depletion continue unchanged, the limits to growth on this planet will be reached sometime within the next one hundred years. The most probable result will be a rather sudden and uncontrollable decline in both population and industrial capacity.... The collapse occurs because of nonrenewable resource depletion. The industrial capital stock grows to a level that requires an enormous input of resources. In

the very process of that growth, it depletes a large fraction of the resource reserves available. As resource prices rise and mines are depleted, more and more capital must be used for obtaining resources, leaving less to be invested for future growth. Finally, investment cannot keep up with depreciation, and the industrial base collapses, taking with it the service and agricultural systems, which have become dependent on industrial inputs (such as fertilizers, pesticides, hospital laboratories, computers, and especially energy for mechanization)...population finally decreases when the death rate is driven upward by lack of food and health services. The exact timing of these events is not meaningful...however, growth is stopped well before the year 2100.

The authors of the report stressed that they couldn't pin down all the variables in their model. Like us, they didn't know the full extent of the Earth's resources and couldn't predict what technological advances might be made in the future. But even under the most generous assumptions, however, they found no scenario that would let civilization survive intact past 2100. Therefore, they urged the world to start the gradual process of moving from growth toward a sustainable economy and population level.

The Limits to Growth should have been a wake-up call, and the five trends it predicted have unfolded largely as predicted. But after attracting initial attention, the report fell out of favor and became widely derided. The reasons had a lot more to do with human psychology than scientific objections.

For one thing, the report offended certain prejudices held by certain groups—for instance, religious conservatives disliked its recommendation that the world's population be kept at a sustainable level through universal access to birth control. And the idea that economic growth should be reined in sounded to some like an attack on the American dream, especially in an era when the Soviet Union was America's top enemy.

It also suffered from being widely misquoted. Many who wrote about it were under the false impression that it claimed oil would run out by 2000, not 2100, as the report actually projected. Since it seemed clear that oil would still be flowing by 2000, this was enough for them to ridicule the entire report.

The year after the report was released witnessed the start of the 1970s oil crisis. At first many people took this as confirming the report's validity. But when oil prices eventually fell, the decline was used to discredit the report and to embarrass its supporters, and the general consensus became that we don't need to worry at all about resources or make any efforts to limit growth. And during the bull market of the 1990s, with oil prices stable at much lower prices than today, most people quickly dismissed anyone who predicted that the situation would change within a decade.

Denial Past and Present

Denial is a common response to the prospect of any unpleasant change, no matter how irrational it seems to anyone who sees reality more clearly. In hindsight, it seems quite unbelievable that in June 1941 most Americans didn't view Hitler as a threat to the world. It took Pearl Harbor to get us into the war at all.

Today, although the notion of Peak Oil has moved from the fringe to the mainstream, Americans still remain very much in denial about its implications. Rather than acknowledge that resources truly are growing scarce, our leaders look for scapegoats and propose faux solutions. The dramatic rise in commodity prices in the first half of 2008 triggered very little debate over the real long-term supply problems. Rather, most of the commentary revolved around the extent to which the gains constituted a speculative bubble.

Mass denial was even more apparent in how our leaders and the media reacted to oil prices shooting well above $100 a barrel. No one, as far as we know, pointed to statements in April 2008 from both Russian and Saudi Arabian officials that indicated those countries had reached or were close to reaching the limits of their ability to produce. This to us reflects utter denial of the reality that oil supplies won't be able to meet future demand. It's as if everyone is simply too scared to face the ramifications of these comments, for to accept them would be to admit the world has changed dramatically, and that we can't proceed with business as usual.

Wall Street has been in denial as well, as evidenced, among other things, by the way it has undervalued oil stocks. The best measure of a company's projected growth is its price-earnings ratio, or P/E. The higher the P/E, the faster growth is expected to be. What is remarkable is that the P/E ratios of energy stocks have actually declined over the past several years. Although most energy stocks have been strong performers, that performance has come from strong earnings growth, not from how Wall Street has valued those earnings. And while you could argue that lower P/Es might be justified for the oil producers, because it will be hard for them to increase production, you can't make the same case for oil service companies, whose business will grow substantially in coming years as the search for oil frantically accelerates. Yet their P/Es have dropped as well.

These dismissive valuations for oil stocks go hand in hand with Wall Street's forecasts for oil itself. *Between 1999 and 2008, oil prices rose more than tenfold.* But at no point during that period was any Wall Street firm projecting that oil prices were in a long-term uptrend. The one that came closest, Goldman Sachs, which garnered a lot of attention for forecasting $100 and $200 oil, continues to maintain that oil would eventually retreat to "normalized" levels some 50 percent below its peak.

(Incidentally, our two previous books—*The Oil Factor* and *The Coming Economic Collapse*—put us on record for having been at least a year ahead of Goldman Sachs in projecting first $100 and then $200 oil. The difference is that we don't think oil will stop at $200, absent a major depression or some other cataclysm. To be fair, in 2007 and 2008, two major firms did begin projecting longer-term uptrends in oil, though neither was American.)

Could Global Warming Save Us?

Interestingly, while most Americans, from Main Street to Wall Street to Washington, D.C., seemingly don't know or accept that the world is truly running low on oil and other essential resources, many are very concerned about another trend: global warming. Global warming encompasses the theory that man-made greenhouse gas emissions, which arise from the burning of fossil fuels, will, if left unchecked, lead to catastrophic changes in the world's climate. Eventually, it will cause sea levels to rise, flooding coastal cities; severe hurricanes will become more frequent; and there will be unprecedented droughts and ecological damage.

Global warming has become part of the zeitgeist, gaining wide acceptance among the general public thanks to a worldwide environmental movement that has grown over the past thirty years. Recently, bestselling books such as Jared Diamond's *Collapse* and Al Gore's Academy Award–winning documentary *An Inconvenient Truth*—not to mention his receipt of the Nobel Prize—have added to the perception that global warming is a serious problem. It is accepted as such by most of the world's scientists, and certainly, with agreements such as the Kyoto Protocol, the international community has moved closer to addressing global warming than it has Peak Commodities.

The two intersect, of course, because efforts to slow global warming all revolve around cutting our use of fossil fuels by a combination of conservation and the development of renewable, green energies. Which leads to the thought that a coordinated, global assault on global warming might be an effective backdoor means of addressing Peak Oil and Peak Commodities.

Perhaps it will be. However, we tend to think that in the end, global warming won't prove enough of a catalyst. For one thing, we may actually be on the verge of a shorter-term drop in global temperatures. At least that's a theory offered in the May 2008 issue of *Nature*, where it was pointed out that it is normal for several years of rising temperatures to be followed by several years of cooling. Such a short-term drop in temperatures wouldn't disprove a longer-term warming trend, but it might put the issue of global warming on the back burner and provide ammunition to those who want to debunk it. And in any case, even without such a cool spell, the most dangerous effects of global warming won't be felt for decades, too far away to make most people willing to take more than the most superficial of actions to forestall it.

In other words, even though more people tend to believe in global warming, the phenomenon of denial is alive and well here, too, as was shown in a study done in 2000 by a team of European researchers. The researchers used focus groups to assess people's attitudes toward climate change. The study first looked at how people felt about reducing their energy consumption. In theory, they were all for it, perceiving a lower-energy lifestyle as positive and desirable and the mark of a world that was friendly and safe for children.

But when it came down to actually switching to a low-energy lifestyle, almost no one was ready to do so. They reconciled this contradiction by resorting to four broad categories of denial. First, to explain why they were unwilling to give up their own personal comfort—for example, to trade their car for a bicycle—they argued that such actions wouldn't really help much. Second, they invoked what is called the "managerial fix interpretation." That is, people argued that the problem really should be solved by government regulations or by new technologies, rather than by individual action.

Third, people argued against changing their own behavior because they didn't trust the government to match their efforts with a sound program addressing the problem. They feared that the government either was incompetent or would be swayed by lobbies pushing in another direction.

The final form of denial pertained to a famous analogy known as the Tragedy of the Commons. Described by Garrett Hardin in 1968, it postulates a pasture, or commons, where everyone in the community is allowed to graze as many cattle as they own. This raises a dilemma: on the one hand, it is in each person's interest to raise as many cattle as possible. On the other, too many cattle will result in overgrazing and the destruction of the entire pasture.

It would make sense to limit the total number of cows to a level that would preserve the pasture's long-term health. However, for each individual herder, each cow he adds to his herd increases his own near-term profit. The damage from one more cow seems insignificant, since it is shared equally by the whole village and the degradation might be noticed only after many years.

Moreover, the herder assumes that even if he refrains from adding more cows, his neighbors won't be so honorable. He concludes that sacrificing his profit won't stop the destruction of the pasture, it will only let his neighbors grow richer at his expense.

Everyone in the village, therefore, ignores the long-term damage to the pasture and gets as big a herd as possible. The result:

the pasture is quickly destroyed, to everyone's ruin. As Hardin puts it, "natural selection favors the forces of psychological denial. The individual benefits as an individual from his ability to deny the truth even though society as a whole, of which he is a part, suffers."

The Tragedy of the Commons rationale shows up in discussions of both global warming and resource shortages. Individuals are reluctant to switch to a low-energy lifestyle because their personal sacrifice would have too big an impact on their own lifestyle and too small an impact on the world. And with no guarantee that everyone else will do their part, there's no incentive at all to act.

Nations, too, can exhibit this kind of thinking. *How could anyone, for instance, convince China to keep its energy use in check if the United States won't do the same?* Why should Americans give up their SUVs (except to save money on gas) if Indians are building massive fleets of cheap cars with no emission controls?

The Upside to Disaster

With human beings so clever at finding ways to remain in denial, it may take a true disaster of some kind or another to get us to face the threat of Absolute Peak Oil and Absolute Peak Commodities, just as it took Pearl Harbor to bring the United States into World War II. Such an event, for instance, might be an attack on a major oil facility. If the Saudis' oil infrastructure were destroyed, to raise one mind-boggling thought, oil production would suddenly fall short of demand by 7 million to 9 million barrels a day. The prices of all commodities would hit new heights, though later they'd likely collapse as the world entered a depression. The entire global economy would fall. The U.S. could survive only through a combination of strategic reserves and rationing.

In the midst of such a global depression, the leaders of the major world economies would have to come together and decide on a program for parceling out whatever energy supplies were left. The top priority would be to use the world's remaining oil and other energy sources to build the global infrastructure to support alternative energy. In the wake of this program, inflation would likely run rampant and our standard of living would decline dramatically. But in the end we might have implemented the global system of alternative energies that we need.

Another possible crisis that could serve as a catalyst could be a policy mistake by the Federal Reserve. As we'll discuss later, we don't think the Fed will risk trying to squelch inflation because of the possibility that such action could trigger a recession that would spiral out of control. And we're not rooting for such an event. Still, if the Fed did miscalculate, it could be another route bringing us into global depression. In this case it would lead to sharply lower demand for oil and other commodities, with prices falling rapidly. The economic slack created might make it easier to build alternative energy infrastructure, and if our political system survived the stress, the depression could set the stage for a massive new works program similar to that in the Great Depression. This time, though, we'd be putting people to work building a new energy infrastructure.

All the above is speculative, of course. And we hope that we can somehow find a way to overcome denial and confront the threat of Absolute Peak Oil and Absolute Peak Commodities without needing a major disaster to get us there. Even under the most favorable possible circumstance, there will be enough pain and dislocation in making the transition to new sources of energy. Let's hope we can do it with less pain rather than more—but above all, let's do it.

PART III

ECONOMIC TSUNAMI

CHAPTER 12

The Inflation Bomb

In July 2008, the inflation rate, as measured by the Consumer Price Index (CPI), reached 5.6 percent. That may not seem excessive, but it is twice the 2 to 3 percent rate targeted by most Western governments and the highest since January 1991. Worse, the Producer Price Index (PPI), which measures the prices received by domestic producers, reached 9.8 percent, the highest rate since 1980–81 and dangerously close to double digits. (We should point out that changes in the PPI often foreshadow similar movements in the CPI.)

Of course, we had been expecting higher inflation for some time. With the price of oil having risen more than tenfold since the late 1990s and most other commodity prices having doubled, it seemed inevitable that, as resource costs became a more important part of the economy, we would eventually reach the point where continued gains would start to drive the inflation rate higher.

Here's how the process works. Imagine a raw material that accounts for just 1 percent of the total cost of a car. When that material doubles in price, it results in only a 1 percent increase in automobile prices. No big deal. Few customers will let such a tiny amount affect their decision to buy a car.

However, if the cost of the material continues rising, so that it eventually accounts for 10 percent of the total cost, then the next time the material price doubles, automobile prices increase by 10 percent. That's a much more noticeable difference, one that will cause some customers to think twice.

And so it is with resources. In the early part of the decade, rising resource prices did not make much difference because resources were a very minor factor in overall economic activity. But that changed in 2008. Once oil prices surpassed $100 a barrel and energy costs rose to 10 percent of GDP in the United States, additional increases in the cost of energy and other resources started to have a major effect on inflation.

Ironically, when commodities corrected during 2008, policy makers and economists, always anxious to put a positive spin on the economy, were quick to predict slower inflation. Yet, in doing so, they actually admitted that resources had become the driving force behind inflation. From now on, as resource prices go, so goes inflation. With global economic growth continuing, putting ongoing pressure on commodities, we can hope for little more than brief periods of inflationary relief. Overall, inflation will spiral out of control, causing our cost of living to ascend to an unbearable height.

However, commodities will not be our only problem. *For some time, the United States has been partially sheltered from the real impact of higher commodity prices because American companies were able to outsource production and services to the developing world, where wages are considerably lower.* That move helped reduce the prices of goods and services in the U.S. However, the advantage gained by outsourcing will soon come to an end. Inflation will further accelerate as we are hit by another vicious circle.

The Wage-Commodity Vicious Circle

Material costs are just one part of the inflation equation. The other aspect that is important to consider is wages. As consumer prices rise, American workers will certainly put pressure on employers to raise wages in line with inflation. However, that pressure will be minor compared to the demands of workers in the developing world who produce the commodities and goods we import. People who are poor to start with simply cannot tolerate large price increases in the staples of life without a corresponding increase in income.

Of course, workers in the developing world want a lot more than to merely keep pace with inflation. For the vast majority of them, economic growth means one thing: a chance to escape from poverty and provide a happy life for their families. While an American family whose income rises from $70,000 to $90,000 a year may see only a slight gain in their lifestyle, there is no doubt that a Chinese family whose annual income jumps from $800 to $4,000 a year will have achieved an immense improvement in their happiness, comfort, and security. For people who lack the essentials of life, more is undeniably better. Not surprisingly, once such people get a taste of more, they utterly refuse to give it up.

Wages in the poorer countries are currently less than one-fifth that of the world average, but they are rising as a result of economic growth as well as higher commodity prices. As they do, so will the cost of all the manufactured goods America imports, and the U.S. CPI as well.

As wages rise in the developing world, so will consumption, and that will drive commodity prices even higher. In other words, we face not only the commodity-energy vicious circle outlined in earlier chapters, but also a wage-commodity vicious circle. The combination of both these circles will help push inflation to ultrahigh levels.

When Growth Turns Bad

Earlier we pointed out that many economic commentators today espouse the virtues of growth. They also assume that growth in the developing world will not adversely affect standards of living in the developed world. Certainly, that has been the case so far, and if commodity supplies were unlimited, it might continue to be true. But since all of humanity is forced to share the world's limited pool of natural resources, strong growth in one part of the world will eventually limit growth elsewhere. As this unfolds, nations blessed with enough natural resources to meet their needs will have an advantage over those that rely on imported commodities.

In the growing competition for resources, the United States finds itself at a disadvantage. *Less than a decade ago, we were importing 60 percent of the industrial metals we consumed. The rest were produced within the U.S. Today we import almost 80 percent.* At one time, we produced all the oil we consumed. Now we import 60 percent of it from other nations. So far, our best sources for commodities have been undeveloped nations. These are the nations that have more resources than they consume, so they can export the rest. But how long will this situation last? As we indicated in chapter 4, not long.

It's easy to imagine a Tom Clancy novel in which a small group of CIA operatives scheme to prevent peace in the Middle East. After all, if a lasting peace were ever achieved in that region, it would be a disaster for the West. Certainly, capitalism and democracy would get a firmer foothold during peacetime. But that's just the problem. Capitalism and peace would lead to economic growth. If the oil-producing nations of the Middle East grew to the point that they were using all of their oil to sustain their own economies, where could the developed nations turn to for oil?

Consider, for example, Iran and the controversy over its nuclear program. Because Iran is OPEC's second-largest oil exporter, most people assume it has all the energy it needs. Therefore, they conclude that the only motivation Iran could have for building nuclear reactors must be to create fuel for nuclear weapons.

However, it's not that clear-cut. Iran's economy is growing by 4.3 percent a year, which means its energy consumption is rising. Roger Stern of Johns Hopkins University analyzed the growth of Iran's domestic energy demand, the depletion rate of its oil production, the cost of raising production, and other factors ("The Iranian Petroleum Crisis and United States National Security," *Proceedings of the National Academy of Sciences* 104.1, January 2, 2007: 377–82). He found that under even the most optimistic scenario, Iran's oil exports will decline to zero by 2015. The Iranian government depends on revenue from oil exports. Therefore, the country has a good reason for wanting nuclear reactors. By using nuclear power to meet its domestic energy needs, Iran hopes it can continue selling oil. Otherwise, it will become a net importer.

If Iran can run out of oil to export, so can every OPEC member. Most Middle East countries are classified as developing nations. So are many other resource-rich countries. We can expect their energy and commodity needs to increase at a rapid pace for the foreseeable future. Eventually, worldwide growth could lead to a situation where, when the United States goes shopping for the commodities it needs, the entire world says, "Sorry, we have nothing to spare." At that point, our economy and our standard of living would be in serious trouble. We would see inflation higher than ever before experienced.

Our Rude Awakening Beckons

One of the hardest things Americans will have to face in future years is the waning of our economic power. Many of us grew up in the years following the end of the Second World War, when the United States entered a period of economic strength and growing prosperity that continued to the end of the century. The way we see ourselves and our position in the world is very much a product of that history. However, it is important to remember that things have changed quite a bit since 1950.

For instance, in 1950, inflation stood at *minus* 2 percent. A loaf of bread cost $0.14 in most places. Half a gallon of milk cost $0.41, including delivery.

Oil sold for just $2.57 a barrel, and its supply seemed endless. We were by far the world's top oil-producing country. A shortage of industrial raw materials was similarly unimaginable.

The United States was practically the only developed nation to emerge from World War II with its manufacturing infrastructure largely undamaged, and that gave it a decisive advantage over other nations. Consequently, Wall Street was the center of the financial universe in 1950. Only speculators invested overseas. On a typical day, the sleepy Dow moved less than a point, about 0.75.

Asia, as we noted in chapter 4, was little more than a backwater then. There were no imports from China; they were embargoed because of Mao. The most common Japanese import was a tiny umbrella made of bamboo and tissue paper marked MADE IN OCCUPIED JAPAN. Almost all merchandise was marked MADE IN U.S.A. or REG. U.S. PAT. OFF.

The federal government budget showed a surplus in 1950, and our balance of trade was positive. Federal government debt stood at just $255.3 billion. We were the envy of other nations. The almighty dollar would remain supreme as the world's reserve currency for decades to come. We had the financial strength to spend our way out of any problem that came along.

Social Security was a "pay as you go" system, with sixteen people paying in for each recipient. Everyone, even the numerous baby boomers who were just being born, could look forward to a financially secure retirement.

The world was also a lot simpler in 1950. Information technology was in its infancy. There were no credit cards, faxes, cell phones, or World Wide Web. Only fifteen computers had been built in the world, and Xerox was still nine years away from selling its first photocopier. The average person kept his retirement savings in a bank account; stocks and bonds were only for the wealthy elite.

Yes, America's future looked rosy in 1950. Unfortunately, today's reality is vastly different. The world economy is undergoing a major transformation. The United States has lost many of its former advantages, and the nation's finances are in rough shape. The era of prosperity is almost at an end.

It's not just that Peak Commodities and inflation threaten our standard of living. Nor that developing economies are catching up to us. It is that our financial strength has deteriorated to the point where we are less able to deal with the problems confronting us.

Over the past century, we have come to believe we can handle whatever economic problem besets Western civilization. For example, the Great Depression, World War II, and the 1999 crash in technology shares taught the U.S. government that it can solve any deflationary crisis simply by raising the money supply and stimulating the economy with government spending.

Of course, it is one thing to spend money when you have a surplus in the budget or your current level of debt is low to begin with. However, compared to 1950, our nation's financial situation is far more fragile today. Rather than maintain a budget surplus, since the turn of the millennium, the federal government has run some of the largest deficits in history—including $412 billion in 2003.

Meanwhile, the national debt has grown to roughly $9 trillion, an amount that equates to $30,000 for every man, woman, and child. No one ever speaks of trying to pay off this debt anymore. It would be impossible.

But one thing hasn't changed all that much: *even today, Americans still cling by and large to the optimism born in the postwar period. Yet, while we bask in a false sense of security, the rug is being quietly pulled out from under us.* The steps we can take to solve the coming problems are far more limited. And unless we wake up now and act with our remaining strength, the future looks bleak.

The Albatross of Spending

In addition to the two vicious circles already mentioned, one other factor will not only contribute to record high inflation, it will make it difficult for us to fund the development of alternative energies, which are absolutely necessary if we are to counter the arrival of Absolute Peaks. That factor is sharply rising government spending.

We noted before that the U.S. government has already amassed some $9 trillion worth of debt, and that so far this century it has pursued record-high deficit spending. Government spending might be manageable if it was used to stimulate economic growth. In that case, higher tax revenues in the future could be used to repay the debt.

However, basic economics dictate that, if spending does not add to growth (that is, enhance the availability of materials or labor), it will be inflationary. Going forward, there are two areas in which the government will be forced to spend massive amounts of money: defense and entitlements. Neither of these areas will add much to economic growth, but they will contribute to rising inflation.

Regarding defense, even putting aside the issue of terrorism on

American soil, the United States and other nations must increase defense spending in order to maintain access to vital commodities as they grow scarce. Since many resource-rich nations are politically unstable as well as underdeveloped, that fight will most likely involve guns.

A 1999 study by the World Bank notes that countries with valuable resources are four times more likely to experience civil war than resource-poor nations (Paul Collier and Anke Hoeffler, "Justice Seeking and Loot Seeking in Civil War," unpublished paper, Washington, D.C., February 17, 1999). Similarly, an article in *Foreign Affairs* points out that between 1993 and 2006, while the number of civil wars worldwide declined, there was no drop in the number of conflicts in oil-rich nations (Michael L. Ross, "Blood Barrels: Why Oil Wealth Fuels Conflict," 87.3, May-June 2008). Furthermore, the author notes:

> More than a dozen countries in Africa, the Caspian basin, and Southeast Asia have recently become, or will soon become, significant oil and gas exporters. Some of these countries, including Chad, East Timor, and Myanmar, have already suffered internal strife. Most of the rest are poor, undemocratic, and badly governed, which means that they are likely to experience violence as well. On top of that, record oil prices will yield the kind of economic windfalls that typically produce further unrest.

To prevent the violence that could disrupt commodity supplies, the United States will be increasingly forced to use its military to promote stable, U.S.–friendly governments in countries prone to instability. In fact, we see signs of this already. However villainous Saddam Hussein may have been, the Iraq war may have been fought primarily to ensure U.S. access to Iraqi oil.

Apart from actual shooting, securing commodity supplies will require a much larger global network of armed, staffed, and expensive outposts that can support friendly governments and intimidate any nations or nationalist groups who want to exercise greater control over the world's remaining resources. Of course, this network is already partially in place (by some estimates, the United States currently maintains over seven hundred active military sites abroad), but it will need to expand.

Meanwhile, other nations will want to develop their military strength and alliances in order to protect their resources and compete with the West for access to resources outside their political territory. If all this military spending doesn't lead to a new arms race or all-out wars over resources, it will at the very least add considerably to U.S. government deficits.

As for entitlement programs such as Social Security and Medicare, much has been written about the burgeoning need of the government to take care of its aging citizens and the inadequacy of current funding. Just as we cannot skimp on defense, we certainly cannot abandon the huge number of baby boomers who are just now reaching retirement age. Nonetheless, according to the Government Accountability Office (GAO), Social Security and Medicare show unfunded obligations totaling some $40.8 trillion. Add that to federal pension obligations and other debts, and the government is on the hook for nearly $53 trillion. That amount equals 90 percent of the total net worth of American households, or $175,000 for every citizen. If current trends continue, by the year 2040 balancing the federal budget could only be achieved by either cutting federal spending on other areas by 60 percent or doubling taxes—both choices that most people would find unacceptable ("Saving Our Future Requires Tough Choices Today," presentation by David M. Walker, Comptroller General of the

United States, sponsored by the U.S. Government Accountability Office, given at Tallahassee, Florida, January 14, 2008).

Many solutions to this problem have been proposed, but whatever decisions are ultimately made, they will add markedly to the government budget and do little to promote real economic growth. In the end, the only way for the government to fund entitlement and defense spending will be by dramatically increasing its debt. The process will pump massive amounts of dollars into the economy, which will lead to still another vicious circle that drives the value of the U.S. dollar steadily lower.

The Dollar's Downfall

The U.S. dollar is already vulnerable because of our dependency on other nations for basic materials. Out-of-control government spending will foster the perception that the United States is financially irresponsible, making foreigners lose confidence in the dollar. As commodity prices rise, foreigners will want to hold the currencies of resource-rich countries in reserve, rather than U.S. dollars, so they can pay for the commodities they need. If the U.S. inflation rate rises above government bond yields, that would be a good excuse to dump dollars altogether.

In time, the dollar's downward spiral will become self-feeding. A weaker dollar will result in the cost of basic commodities rising faster in the United States than in countries with stronger currencies. The U.S. will become more indebted and still more dependent on others, adding even more pressure to the dollar's descent.

We realize that all of this contrasts with some current thinking on the relationship between the dollar and commodities. Many analysts have argued that the weak dollar is the cause of rising commodity prices. However, the value of the dollar has little or no effect on the scarcity of commodities. Rather, the causality is almost surely reversed. Rising commodity prices weaken commodity-dependent countries and strengthen those that are resource rich. For further proof, witness how the currencies of commodity-based countries such as Australia, Brazil, and Canada have gained in recent years.

One more nail on the coffin: at a certain point in the dollar's descent, OPEC and other commodity producers will stop pricing their wares in U.S. dollars. Instead, they will elect to price commodities in terms of a basket of currencies—which will likely include gold. Once the dollar loses its status as a reserve currency, its decline will accelerate, and so will inflation.

Finally, remember that in addition to this backdrop we will still need to fund a massive program to develop alternative energies. Assuming we launch such an effort in time, it will place yet another burden on government spending, pushing inflation still higher. On the upside, it would offer hope of light at the end of the tunnel. For if the effort succeeds in developing viable, affordable alternatives, energy prices will ultimately start to fall, with a ripple effect on prices of other commodities—a virtuous rather than vicious circle.

Nonetheless, achieving a sustainable and sufficient energy supply could take decades. Meanwhile, we expect that within a few short years, inflation will hit unprecedented heights. People will be looking back with longing at the 10 to 15 percent annual inflation of the 1970s. The cruel new reality will be 30 to 40 percent. Such an environment, characterized by a rapidly climbing cost of living and declining value of investments, will be extremely harsh for anyone who is unprepared.

CHAPTER 13

Inflation: Why the Old Solutions Will No Longer Work

You may feel at this point that we are being too flat-out pessimistic. After all, the United States has faced energy shortages and double-digit inflation before, most recently in the 1970s and early 1980s, and we managed to pull through in the end. Inflation was tamed, oil prices fell, and the stage was eventually set for the biggest bull market in history. However, when you look at how those earlier crises were resolved, it becomes clear that what worked then isn't going to bail us out today.

One difference is that during the energy crises of the 1970s, the world retained the ability to increase supplies of oil and other commodities. The supply-demand squeeze wasn't permanent, because it stemmed largely from politics. In 1973, OPEC imposed an oil embargo to punish the nations that had supported Israel in the Yom Kippur War, and the cartel decided to force world oil prices higher in general. In 1979–80, a second oil crisis resulted when the Iranian Revolution and the Iran-Iraq War disrupted Iran's oil output. However, there was still plenty of affordable oil in the ground. Throughout the entire period, the world maintained at least 20 to 30 percent excess production capacity for oil and virtually all other commodities. Once the political situation improved, oil supplies could rise again. True, Iranian production took time to restart, but new fields in Alaska and the North Sea came online in the late 1970s and early 1980s and helped take up the slack, and prices came back down.

Another difference is that in the 1970s and early 1980s, falling demand in the United States was enough to have an impact on prices. Demand can fall on its own as a commodity becomes more expensive. Certainly, soaring oil prices in the 1970s encouraged some conservation to take place. President Carter installed solar panels and a woodstove in the White House and appeared on television wearing a sweater to set an example for all Americans. We started building cars with greater fuel efficiency (until we replaced them years later with SUVs) and turning down thermostats at night. Oil consumption in the U.S. fell from a peak of 18.8 million barrels a day in 1978 to a low of 15.2 million in 1983. As individuals sought to save money on their gasoline and electric bills, the resulting decline in energy consumption, together with the increase in supplies, helped bring energy prices and inflation down.

A Hamstrung Fed

However, most of the credit for lowering demand and taming inflation goes to Federal Reserve Chairman Paul Volcker's action on the monetary front. In the early 1980s, Volcker decided to halt inflation, even if that meant killing economic growth at the same time. He targeted money supply growth at a noninflationary rate and let interest rates reach whatever level was consistent. The federal funds rate rose to 21.5 percent, well above the inflation rate high of 14.6 percent, and the economy, by many measures, fell into the worst recession since the Great Depression. The unemployment rate, for example, hit double digits. So it took a lot of pain, but Volcker's plan worked. The drop in consumption ushered in a generation of declining inflation and historically strong performance from the financial markets.

Today, however, the situation is very different, and there is no chance that we could take similar measures to halt inflation. *What worked in the 1970s will not work this time around.*

In the first place, the factors driving inflation higher today are not so easily dispelled. The approach of Peak Oil and Peak Commodities results not from transitory political upsets but rather are systemic problems with no easy answers. We have already discussed why it will be difficult, if not impossible, to raise worldwide oil production from now on. Spare production capacity is already virtually nonexistent. There are no big fields like the North Sea waiting to be brought online—at least not unless oil prices race closer to the $200 mark. The only country that might be able to raise its production of inexpensive oil is Iraq. But if the fighting in Iraq were to end tomorrow, it still would take many years for Iraq's output to reach full capacity. Even then, the increase would likely amount to a mere drop in the proverbial bucket.

And second, the Federal Reserve doesn't have the same leeway today to engineer a recession and thereby curb consumption and lower prices for oil and commodities. Events in recent years have shown us that such a plan would cause more harm today than even skyrocketing inflation. There are two reasons why: debt and the developing world.

The United States today is a nation of debtors. As the chart on page 152 illustrates, debt levels as a percentage of GDP are at highs not seen since the Great Depression, and they have maintained a steady and relentless uptrend. One major cause is the coming of age of the baby boom generation. When these folks settled down in the early 1980s, they borrowed large amounts of money to

Debt as Percentage of GDP

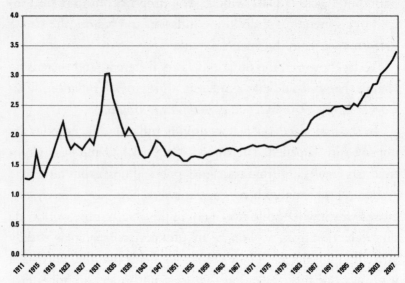

Sources: Federal Reserve, The Complete Investor *(Stephen Leeb, editor)*

acquire all the necessities and luxuries of life—including, most significantly, homes. Moreover, government and business debt also has been rising sharply.

These high debt levels cripple the Federal Reserve's ability to battle inflation because they make engineering a recession far too risky a proposition. One effect of a recession is to make it harder for consumers and businesses to pay off debt; since they have less money coming in, more individuals are unemployed, while business profits are slumping. In an economy where debt is high, a recession that lasts too long or is too severe could lead to mass bankruptcies, causing the whole economy to come crashing down. Moreover, high debt levels make it extremely difficult for the Fed to reel in a recession if one ever begins.

The Fed's actions during the 2001 recession, which followed the crash in technology shares and the 9/11 terrorist attacks, are revealing. The slowdown was relatively minor, lasting only a few

Fed Funds Rate

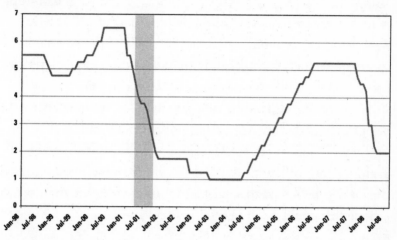

Shaded areas indicate U.S. recessions as determined by the National Bureau of Economic Research.
Source: Bloomberg

months—one of the shortest recessions on record—and having virtually no effect on consumer demand, which continued to rise throughout the duration. Still, the Federal Reserve responded with an extraordinary easing of monetary policy. The ten-year chart of the federal funds rate shows that, in 2001, interest rates fell to roughly 1 percent. This aggressive response on the Fed's part to a mild recession wasn't overkill. Rather, it was an acknowledgment that the huge debt levels overhanging the economy could make even a mild recession turn vicious in very short order.

One of the Fed's major goals was to make sure home prices didn't collapse. Home mortgages represent the biggest chunk of consumer debt, and homes are far more leveraged today than in the 1980s; back then, home mortgages were only 27 percent of the value of homes, compared to 40 percent today. Dramatic declines in housing prices, therefore, today more than ever have the potential to rip through the entire economy, leading to a rise in consumer bankruptcies as people find their most valuable asset—their home—is suddenly worth a lot less. Such bankruptcies, in turn, are a direct threat to banks, most of which have lent significantly more money than they hold. The final domino is the corporate sector, which depends on banks and is highly leveraged itself. *In short, a collapse in home prices leads to economic chaos.*

As a result, the Federal Reserve can't do anything that risks bringing on a decline in housing prices, which means that engineering a recession, as Volcker did, is off the table. In any battle against rising inflation, the Fed has lost its chief weapon. And thus it will be forced to surrender to inflation rather than take a chance that could result in economic collapse.

Derivatives and Inflation

Further complicating matters are the increasingly complex ways in which financial debt is structured today. The collapse of Bear Stearns in the fallout of the subprime mortgage crisis that began in August 2007 is a case in point. Following the interest rate cuts of the early 2000s, the excess liquidity thereby created led to an environment where taking on unwarranted risks became the new norm. This was especially true in the housing sector, where loans were available for the asking with almost no down payment. Wall Street and the banks couldn't have cared less that these loans were often given to individuals with poor credit—the now infamous subprime borrowers—because the wonders of financial engineering (read financial complexity) concealed the risks. The subprime loans were bundled together with high-quality debt instruments. These new, complex debt instruments, which by and large included more good debt than risky debt, were highly rated by the rating institutions.

The problem was that the presumed quality of these debt instruments rested on the assumption that housing prices would never fall. And relatedly, the financial community failed to consider what might occur if interest rates rose, which they did.

And what happened then? Chaos broke out. Many of the subprime borrowers who had taken out large adjustable rate mortgages found they couldn't keep up with the payments. The resulting increase in defaults and decline in home prices was bad enough in itself. However, the losses became exponentially greater because of the role played by derivatives, the epitome of financial complexity.

It turned out these risky mortgages had been packaged into mortgage-backed securities (MBSs), sliced up and sold as collateralized debt obligations (CDOs), and bought on margin by hedge funds or used as collateral in extremely complex schemes designed to make a lot of money for Wall Street firms.

As we noted, the one thing financial institutions did not plan on when they were creating this huge derivatives position was the possibility that home prices could fall. When home prices did indeed fall, those derivatives turned out to be worth $210 billion less than previously thought.

The balance sheets of banks and mortgage lenders around the world were heavily damaged as a result of the subprime crisis, which has had multiple repercussions. These include the demise of Lehman Brothers, the failure of Bear Stearns, and the fact that Goldman Sachs and Morgan Stanley shed their rarefied status as investment bankers to become full-service banks.

The subprime crisis taught the Federal Reserve an indelible lesson: in an economy saddled with debt that is in turn leveraged with complex financial instruments such as derivatives (which by some estimates now total some $681 trillion), curbing the rise of inflation is a dangerous business. Any serious attempt to do so by raising interest rates and tightening money supplies risks sending the economy into a severe recession—possibly a second Great

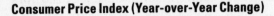

Consumer Price Index (Year-over-Year Change)

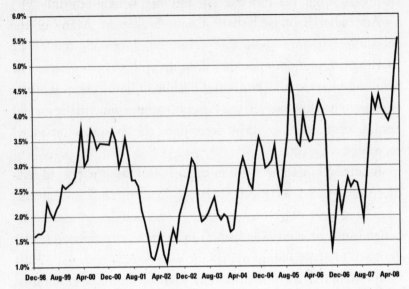

Source: Bloomberg

Depression—in which the hardship would be catastrophic. Federal Reserve Chairman Ben Bernanke, an expert on the first Great Depression of the 1930s, has made it clear that the last thing he wants is a replay of that event. Out-of-control inflation will be hard enough for the American public to bear, but a depression would be far more damaging.

Clearly, by 2008 the Federal Reserve had realized how vulnerable the U.S. economy had become. When the economy began to slow down once more, the Fed abandoned any effort to control inflation and launched yet another very aggressive stimulation program. In fact, compared to its more measured response to earlier crises, its actions show just how fearful of recession the Fed has become.

Consider the difference between the Federal Reserve's actions in the subprime crisis of 2008 and those of 1990. In both years, a real estate downturn led to economic malaise. And both times the Federal Reserve lowered interest rates—or specifically, the discount rate—in order to stimulate the economy and prevent a downward spiral.

However, in 1990, the Fed delayed taking action until the end of the year, when all the hard data clearly said the economy was in a recession. In 2008, the Federal Reserve felt it was too dangerous to wait for any hard data, such as unemployment insurance claims, to confirm the downturn. Instead, it jammed its foot on the monetary accelerator in a preemptive strike, flooding the market with liquidity. Short-term interest rates fell by more than half and many monetary aggregates were expanding at record or near record rates.

Particularly striking is how fast the broadest measure of the money supply, known as M3, rose. The government stopped publishing data on M3 in recent years. (Some speculate the reason was to conceal just how fast the money supply is growing.) Fortunately, various economists still compute it. According to their calculations, M3 rose faster during this period than at any time in modern history, at a rate of roughly 17 percent annually! Extraordinarily, this aggressive easing of monetary policy took place while commodity prices were in a strong uptrend and inflation was rising to pre-1990 levels.

Further evidence that the federal government won't risk a recession and the drop in home prices that it would cause comes from the recent extraordinary purchase by the government of mortgage giants Freddie Mac and Fannie Mae. Freddie Mac and Fannie Mae together carry more than 50 percent of home mortgages in the United States, amounting to $5.4 trillion. The bailout of these two firms shows clearly the federal government knows that supporting home prices is an overriding priority.

The bottom line: the Federal Reserve and federal government are determined to avoid a recession at all costs. But they can't serve two masters at once. Having decided they can't risk a serious recession, they've lost their only real tool for curbing inflation.

The Loss in U.S. Clout

Besides, it is doubtful a Volcker-type recessionary campaign would work anyway today because of all the ways in which the world economy has changed since the 1980s. In 1980, the United States was still the world's economic powerhouse. A recession in the U.S. had a huge impact on the global economy. Back then, "when the U.S. sneezed, the world caught a cold." It would infect worldwide growth, causing it to falter, and commodity prices and inflation would snap into line.

Of course, even then, commodity consumption continued to rise in the developing countries. (That was true even for oil, despite prices having risen twentyfold since their low of the previous decade.) But in those days, developing nations comprised just a small fraction of the world economy, so their rising consumption had very little effect on the global supply-demand balance.

Today, however, as we noted in chapter 4, GDP in the developing world has actually surpassed that of the developed world, and the developing world consumes more oil than the developed world. With the developing world now an equal or greater player on the world's economic stage, a recession in the developed world would have less of an impact on the world's economy and hence on commodity prices.

Nor can we expect the developing world to conserve resources, even as prices rise. In developing economies, growth is achieved only by raising consumption. They simply are not in a position to conserve commodities unless growth turns down, and the implication of negative growth in the developing world is pretty horrible to consider.

Bear in mind that about 40 percent of people in the developing world survive on $2 a day or less. They simply could not tolerate a decline in their incomes. Also, in much of the developing world, and perhaps especially in China, high growth is necessary to provide new jobs for workers migrating to urban areas. Without rapid growth, unemployment would rise sharply. A real downturn in developing economies would therefore put more than just the economy in danger. Civil unrest would likely result. The whole social fabric could unravel. Many places could see a return to another form of government or economic management.

Creating such a devastating recession in the developing world would be the only way to reduce global consumption today. For the Federal Reserve, engineering a U.S. recession big enough to spread to the developing world would be a very tall order. In fact, such a recession would be better called a catastrophic depression. We doubt the Fed has either the courage or the stupidity to try such a plan. It would be equivalent to the United States committing economic suicide. Ergo, we don't think it will happen—other than by some accident—and therefore we think high and rising inflation will be the dominant economic backdrop in coming years.

Inflation, Depression, and Absolute Peaks

If high inflation is a virtual certainty in coming years, there are various ways in which it may unfold. Some of these potential scenarios would be more tolerable than others, but none are good, and they all involve considerably more suffering than the United States experienced in the 1970s and early 1980s. We label them bad, worse, and worst. As we go through them, keep in mind that whichever scenario develops, it will both impact and be impacted by the vicious circles among resource shortages.

Given the choices, the "bad"—that is, best—scenario would be for inflation to climb fairly steadily, which would happen if the Fed does its job and wards off recession. Of course, there could continue to be relatively minor periods of slowing growth, such as occurred in 2001 and 2008, which would bring the inflation rate down slightly. But each slowdown would only set the stage for a new stretch of even more rapid inflation. That's because each time the economy slowed, it would inhibit the development of new energy and commodity supplies. Thus, when growth resumed, commodity prices would move higher and growth, because of less access to commodities, would be weaker.

The economy would experience a slow but fairly steady increase in inflation, much like a frog being slowly boiled in water. If you put a frog in cold water and raise the temperature gradually, the frog will die before it realizes what is happening. Similarly, we won't recognize how serious the situation is until inflation reaches unheard-of levels—perhaps 30 or 40 percent in the developed world.

Things would be even graver, however, if the Fed, deciding after all to take a stab at controlling inflation through tighter money, set off more than a mild recession—our "worse" scenario. A serious slowdown could morph into a period of deflation in which unemployment rises and prices fall—including, most seriously, home prices. As we pointed out in our previous book, *The Coming Economic Collapse*, "if home prices suddenly started to fall, the result would easily be the vicious circle to end all vicious circles."

The reason, as we discussed before, are today's high debt levels. In 1981, Americans' household debt stood at roughly $1.4 trillion. Today it is nearly $14 trillion—a tenfold increase. In 1981, the average American household spent less than 11 percent of its income on servicing debts. Today, it spends 14 percent. The subprime crisis was bad enough, in that it brought home prices down 17 percent from their peak (according to the Case-Shiller Home Price Index). Had the Federal Reserve not acted preemptively to prevent a serious recession, unemployment would have risen significantly, consumer spending would have plummeted, and mortgage delinquency rates would have surged much higher as unemployed people fell behind on their payments. Consequently, home prices might have suffered a much more serious collapse.

A full-scale collapse in home prices would be a far greater disaster than a crash in the stock market. Again, to quote *The Coming Economic Collapse*:

> Consider the technology bubble for a moment. In 2000, stocks represented more wealth than homes. So you might assume that if we survived a major decline in stock prices, we could survive a similar decline in home prices. Unfortunately, survival would not be so easy with home prices falling. Declining home prices would also mean a slumping economy and slumping stocks.... The average person has more wealth tied up in his or her home than in the stock market.... With home prices, stock prices, and the economy all slumping, all feeding on one another, it would indeed be a vicious circle.

Saving the economy from such a vicious circle would take more extreme measures than were needed to cope with the bursting of the technology bubble. To continue:

> It would take massive amounts of money.... Government spending would need to reach unimaginably high levels.... If the economy survived, it would emerge with much higher debt levels than before. Moreover, we would

still face the same hideous inflationary problem, a shortage of energy, and the prospect of sharply rising oil prices.

This scenario is like the first on steroids. It would involve much greater swings in the economic growth rate. Some of the economic downturns could temporarily lead to much lower inflation, as declining consumption would reduce commodity prices. However, the consequence would be that no effort would be made to replace depleted mines and oil fields. Exploration would cease. Projects under development would be shut down. Once the Federal Reserve managed to get the economy moving again, growth would likely be slower than the time before. Yet commodity supplies would be much tighter, causing inflation to soar to even more extreme heights than in our first scenario.

Both our "bad" and "worse" scenarios envision jagged uptrends for inflation and jagged downtrends for overall economic growth. In other words, inflation could follow a pattern something like this: rise to 6 percent, fall to 3 percent, rise to 9 percent, fall to 5 percent, rise to 13 percent, fall to 8 percent, and so on. At the same time, the trajectory for growth would be: rise to 4 percent, fall to 1 percent, rise to 3 percent, fall to 0.5 percent, rise to 2 percent, fall to zero, and so on.

The differences between these first two scenarios are simply how great the swings are, and we'd expect that the reality will fall somewhere in between. The determining factor will be how skillfully the Federal Reserve manages its monetary policy. Regardless, the price of every commodity from asphalt to zinc will soar higher with each new bout of inflation. Hold on to your jewelry, hold on to your silverware. A sterling silver teaspoon could eventually be worth more than $500.

The third scenario is utter catastrophe. If the Federal Reserve totally fails at its job, the economy could enter a recession that becomes self-feeding. It could become a depression that dwarfs that of the 1930s, and it could spread to the developing world, wreaking economic collapse and social upheaval. With the world's economies so interdependent, it would be next to impossible to rescue the U.S. economy from such a disaster, and it could mean the end of capitalism and of civilization as we know it. It would not be the first time civilization has fallen, but it would be the worst collapse, because any attempts to start civilization anew would be in a world devoid of easily accessible and harvestable resources.

As we contemplate these alarming possibilities, here is perhaps the most important point of all: if, regardless of how chaotic the economy becomes, we fail to act soon enough to develop sustainable alternative energies and thus slash through the vicious circles of resource shortages, even the seemingly more tolerable scenarios we've outlined ultimately will lead to catastrophe as we reach Absolute Peak Oil and Absolute Peak Commodities. So while the right decisions by the Fed and other governmental entities will make it possible for us to avert the worst-case scenario, they won't ensure that we do. Only the development of alternatives will do that. As we experience the jagged ups and downs in the economy that we foresee, it will be essential to maintain, in the face of ever more severe economic turmoil, an absolutely clear-eyed commitment to alternative energies and an unflagging understanding of just what is at stake.

PART IV

INVESTMENTS FOR A CHAOTIC WORLD

CHAPTER 14

Gold: Your Single Best Bet as the Commodity Crisis Unfolds

In April 2007, the *New York Times* Week in Review ran a political cartoon showing a man, his face hidden, reading a newspaper whose headlines proclaimed, "Iran Takes Hostages...Unrest in the Middle East...Rising Gas Prices." The next panel revealed the man to be former President Carter musing, "I can't wait until the '70s are over."

We have long predicted that, thanks in part to the growing oil squeeze, the 2000s would resemble the 1970s (see, for instance, our 1999 book, *Defying the Market*), particularly with respect to the performance of various investment categories. So far, we have been largely on target. The table on page 168 compares the returns on various investment classes in the 1970s, 1990s, and 2000s. On most counts, the current period has so far had more in common with the 1970s than the 1990s. Both stocks (as measured by the S&P 500) and cash have barely beaten inflation. After taxes, the real returns in both periods have been negative. Meanwhile, small cap stocks have generated solid real returns and, as in the 1970s, have outperformed large caps. Also similar to the 1970s, but not

Comparing Three Decades

	1970s		2000s		1990s	
Asset Class	Nominal Return	Real Return	Nominal Return	Real Return	Nominal Return	Real Return
Cash	6.8	−1.3	3.0	0.5	4.9	2.0
Commodities	11.0	2.9	8.2	5.7	−1.3	−4.2
Crude Oil	26.4	18.3	14.0	11.5	2.7	−0.2
Gold Bullion	33.1	25.0	10.9	8.4	−2.5	−5.4
Gold Stocks	28.0	19.9	12.9	10.4	−4.5	−7.4
Long Bonds	3.9	−4.2	8.6	6.1	8.8	5.9
Oil Service Stocks	31.0	22.9	9.1	6.6	9.4	6.5
Oil Stocks	14.2	6.1	16.0	13.5	9.3	6.4
S&P 500	8.4	0.3	1.1	−1.4	18.2	15.3
Small Caps	17.5	9.4	8.0	5.5	15.1	12.2
CPI	8.1		2.5		2.9	
GDP	3.3		2.6		3.2	

Sources: *Bloomberg, Standard & Poor's,* The Complete Investor *(Stephen Leeb, editor)*

the 1990s, commodities and commodity-related stocks have recently been strong performers, easily beating other asset classes.

Yet, there are some differences as well. Throughout the first part of this decade, the inflation rate stayed lower than in the 1970s. Only in 2008 did it finally rise above an annual rate of 5 percent, for the first time since a brief spike in 1990. By comparison, inflation remained above 5 percent for most of the 1970s. We also note that 5 percent inflation has so far not triggered any alarms. Most of the commentators today have remained astonishingly confident that it cannot last and is not worth worrying about, whereas in 1971 President Nixon considered 4 percent inflation serious enough to warrant an emergency bout of wage and price controls.

We have already discussed the many reasons why inflation will set new records in the near future. The critical question, however, is why inflation has stayed low for so long, despite high liquidity, low interest rates, and strongly rising commodity prices.

Two causes stand out, both of which are nearing the end of their influence. First, labor in the developing world, especially Chindia, has remained cheap, which has helped keep import prices low (and encouraged outsourcing to Asia). A second and subtler reason is that it takes time for commodity prices to rise to the point where they start to control the economy.

For example, the most important commodities are those related to energy. In the 1970s, it was only after energy costs had risen to 8 percent of overall economic output that inflation appeared on the economic radar screen. In the mid-1970s, when energy costs hit 10 percent of GDP, inflation truly started to gallop. Conversely, it wasn't until the mid-1980s, when energy costs fell below 10 percent of GDP, that inflation entered a serious retreat. Moreover, the high point for inflation (1981) was also the time when energy's share of GDP peaked at over 13 percent.

According to the most recent figures from the U.S. Department of Energy, energy expenditures as a share of GDP rose to 8.4 percent in 2005, for the first time since 1989. Unfortunately, the department issues these figures only every three years. However, considering that since 2005 oil prices have gone from around $70 to $130, it is reasonably safe to assume that energy expenditures now make up an even larger percent of GDP and that we have passed the point where commodity prices began dictating inflation levels. So it is not surprising that virtually all measures of inflation are higher today than they were ten years ago.

In addition, the benefit that the United States obtained from taking advantage of inexpensive labor in Asia has probably passed its peak. Wages and inflation are rising strongly in China now, and the undervalued Chinese yuan has begun to gain ground

Consumer (CPI) and Producer (PPI) Inflation (Year-over-Year Change)

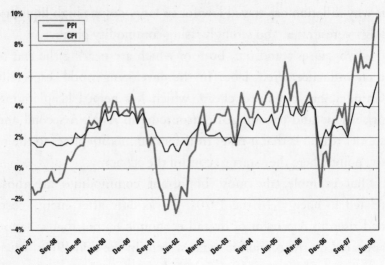

Source: Bloomberg

against the U.S. dollar. So we can safely say that the two factors that have kept inflation under control—energy costs as a relatively low percent of GDP and inexpensive Chinese imports—are both fading. The recent uptick in the level of consumer and producer prices is likely the start of the inflation wave we have been expecting, which means the biggest difference between the 2000s and the 1970s will soon disappear.

The other difference between the 2000s and the 1970s is that so far this decade long-term bonds have been better performers. However, this will surely come to an end as inflation moves seriously higher. A rising inflation rate will cause bond buyers to demand higher yields as compensation, and that will bring bond prices lower. Just as in the 1970s, bonds will shortly become money-losing investments.

Unchecked, the wave of inflation that is rapidly approaching will result in a catastrophic loss of wealth, particularly for middle- and upper-class Americans whose savings are largely invested in financial securities. For many Americans it could dash hopes for a wealthy or even a comfortable retirement.

Fortunately, there are steps you can take that will help you thrive in the years ahead. An investment strategy designed to profit despite (or because of) inflation will help you be among the few to emerge from this period considerably wealthier than today. At the very least, it will help you shield your family from the devastation that is coming. Your first step, however, is to ignore much of the advice doled out by the financial industry. Though it may be well-intentioned, it can lead you horribly astray.

Why Most Financial Advice Today Will Only Make You Poor

Let us review for a moment what happened the last time inflation briefly gained the upper hand. Specifically, imagine it is 1965 and you are a successful executive. You've just turned fifty. You've raised your children, put them through school, and paid off your mortgage. Thanks to your hard work and a disciplined savings plan, you have set aside around $500,000 in savings. Your career is close to its peak, and your health is only just starting to fade. You are now ready to begin planning for a well-earned retirement, one in which you can fulfill all the dreams you postponed while you were working.

In order to have your desired retirement lifestyle, you estimate you need to amass a fund of around a million dollars. The income from this fund will let you maintain this lifestyle for many years, and should cover your future medical expenses. You may even leave a reasonable estate to your children or contribute to your grandchildren's education.

To make sure you do things right, you go to a financial planner for help in investing your $500,000. Any competent adviser back then would have given you virtually the same advice: play it relatively safe. Keep about 50 percent of your money in ultra-secure long-term U.S. government bonds and invest the rest in blue-chip stocks.

Like most financial planners, yours relies on recent history to estimate future returns. So his reasoning is pretty straightforward. Between 1950 and 1965 the returns on bonds had been anemic—about 2 percent a year. After inflation, investors made just a shade above zero in real returns. That's not a great payback. However, your planner reminds you that this is your retirement fund. Safety of capital should be your primary concern. Government bonds are the safest harbor because they guarantee the return of your capital.

As for stocks, the market had gained about 16 percent annually during the same 1950–1965 period. After inflation, investors made 14 percent a year in real returns. So your adviser assumes the stock component of your savings will multiply eightfold by the time you retire in 1981. In other words, the combined returns from stocks and bonds should give you your million-dollar nest egg with reasonably low risk. And there is even room for some disappointment. If stocks were to return just 10 percent during the period, you would still end up with a million dollars in real purchasing power.

Contrary to the assumptions of financial planners, however, the future seldom resembles the recent past. So now let us flash forward to 1981, when you are entering retirement, and see what your investment plan produced.

The period from 1965 to 1981 was much like today. The dollar lost ground. Oil, gold, and commodity prices rose. Stocks turned out to be more volatile than profitable. Most blue-chip averages, such as the Dow, ended up barely changed from mid-1960 levels. After reinvesting dividends, the average annual gain was just under 6 percent—less than half what you expected. Bonds, which move inversely to inflation, were considerably lower in price but yielded much more than they did in the 1960s. Their total annual return—price change plus interest—was actually a touch higher than expected, at 2.5 percent.

But you specifically chose a safe, low-risk investment strategy, one with room for disappointment! Surely you will still be able to retire in comfort? Unfortunately, far from it. The situation is much worse than it appears.

You see, absolute returns are not what really count. Your *real* returns, returns after inflation, are what determine your lifestyle. Obviously, if the amount of money you have doubles, but the price of your dream house goes up threefold, you will have a much harder time paying for it. And that is exactly what happened.

Inflation, which for most of the postwar period through 1965 had rarely risen above 2 percent, averaged about 7 percent since you started investing for retirement, cutting deeply into your real returns. Your savings may have grown by about 4 percent a year, but because the price of food, clothes, and everything else rose an average of 7 percent annually, *you actually lost 3 percent a year in purchasing power.* By the early 1980s, rather than a million dollars in purchasing power, you have only the equivalent of about $300,000—far less than what you started with. Your retirement dream has started to turn to ashes.

Had you been fifteen years older, of course, your situation would have been even worse. Imagine that, in 1965, you had been just entering retirement. You had already socked away as much wealth as you were ever going to in some combination of cash, bonds, and stocks. In that case, you would have spent your retirement years watching your fixed income lose its buying power. Your dream of enjoying a comfortable retirement and leaving a nice legacy to your offspring would have been replaced with a desperate struggle to meet your bills while becoming an ever greater burden on your children.

The years 1965–1981 were actually the worst period ever for investors of all stripes. It is true that stock market averages fell much more in absolute terms in the 1930s. *Nonetheless, after adjusting for inflation, investors actually made more money in the 1930s than in the 1970s.*

As an investor nearing retirement today, you face an even more difficult environment than did those in your parents' generation. Like them, you need a pool of wealth that will see you through to the end of your life (and with medical advances, your life span could be much longer). You may also want to leave something to your heirs. If you assume your investments will earn 10 percent a year, then you will likely need a fund equal to at least ten times your current income to maintain your present lifestyle.

However, that does not take inflation into account. If the inflation rate averages just 2 percent, your real return will only be 8 percent. So to maintain your lifestyle and your capital, your fund must exceed twelve times your annual salary. We say 2 percent because that has been the rate Western governments have targeted for some time, and it is the rate typically assumed by financial planners. *The problem is that, as we write this, inflation has already risen to over 5 percent and is virtually certain to exceed that of the 1970s as oil and commodity supplies grow tighter.*

Consider again the example of our hypothetical 1960s executive. In his case, an average annual inflation rate of 7 percent turned a $500,000 portfolio into one with a buying power of only $300,000. Had inflation averaged just three points higher, to 10 percent, his $500,000 would have shrunk in value to about $200,000. In other words, *a mere 3 percentage-point increase in the inflation rate would have resulted in an additional 33 percent loss of spending power.*

Imagine then the devastation that 20 to 30 percent annual inflation—a result of the growing oil and commodities squeeze—

will inflict on the average person's retirement fund over the next ten years. Clearly, to achieve your retirement dreams, you will either need to amass a retirement fund many times larger or seek considerably higher investment returns (which implies taking on considerably higher risk).

Most investors will find both of these options difficult, though we have some advice that can help you succeed. The only other alternative, however, will be a substantially lower standard of living, and the abandonment of your other financial goals. For the millions of today's investors who fail to take appropriate measures now, that will be their unfortunate fate.

Compounding the problem, once again, will be the advice given out by financial planners. Much as in 1965, today's experts typically advise future retirees to invest in a well-diversified portfolio containing both stocks (meaning the S&P 500) and bonds. However, there is one small difference. Today, the standard advice is that the percentage of bonds in your portfolio should equal your age. For instance, the average sixty-five-year-old is told to put 65 percent of his or her savings into bonds. We already know what happened to investors in 1965 who put 50 percent of their savings in bonds. Inflation affected bonds much more severely than stocks, destroying retirees' purchasing power. Today, those approaching or in retirement are advised to put a much higher portion of their savings into the asset class that will suffer the worst damage. Consequently, the average investor's loss of wealth will be much greater.

The other danger is that both financial planners and the average investor today have been well schooled in the advantages of maintaining a diversified stock portfolio. A principle of Modern Portfolio Theory, which is practiced by virtually every competent financial adviser, states that diversification allows an investor to reap the maximum long-term return for a given level of risk.

However, while diversification is a sound strategy most of the time, it fails utterly during periods of high inflation. As we pointed out, in the 1970s, the S&P 500, which is generally considered to be a safe, diversified basket of blue-chip stocks, one often recommended by financial advisers, actually lost money in real terms. In the even bigger inflationary wave that is coming, following the advice of the typical financial adviser is a formula for disaster. With 20 to 30 percent inflation, a diversified portfolio that tracks the market will likely lose value at an extremely rapid pace in both nominal and real terms. Unless you beat the index by a considerable margin, you will grow steadily poorer. In fact, the average investor will likely suffer a much greater loss of wealth than occurred during either the Great Depression or the 1970s.

Surviving and thriving during the next few years requires a completely different strategy. In the first place, the investors who make fortunes will not be those with diversified portfolios containing a high percentage of bonds. They will be those who concentrate their capital in those industries and investments that can produce good returns despite high inflation. However, it is not that simple.

Adapting to the investment environment of the next few years will require a constant balancing act. As we mentioned earlier, the government will be walking a fine line between fostering growth and trying to contain the damage caused by inflation. It will need to maintain monetary and fiscal policies loose enough to stimulate the economy, while simultaneously tight enough to prevent inflation from rising too quickly and turning into hyperinflation. It will be a tough balance to maintain, and we expect the Federal Reserve and Congress will make occasional mistakes. If the Federal Reserve raises interest rates too quickly or fails to maintain adequate liquidity, a temporary bout of *deflation* would result, in which prices of not just commodities but all assets fall.

Deflationary periods will destroy the average citizen's wealth even faster than inflation. Consumer debt is extremely high today, and if salaries and the value of assets decline, debt burdens will become much more onerous. Consequently, balancing your portfolio to meet alternating periods of rapidly rising prices and declining prices will become a new art. It will be a world even more treacherous than that of the 1970s.

A Juggling Act Worse Than the 1970s

To fully understand how to navigate between inflation and deflation over the next few years, you will first need to apply the lessons learned in the last great inflation wave. Assuming the next ten years will resemble the 1970s but will be more extreme, the first major implication is that you cannot sit on the sidelines with your life savings "safely" tucked away in cash. Cash, in the form of a savings or checking account, will not earn nearly enough interest to compensate you for the decline in its purchasing power brought about by inflation (never mind the fact that the government will tax you on the interest you earn).

In the same way, bonds will no longer be a free ride. Already, the real return from short-term U.S. Treasuries has turned negative, which gives you very little reason to own them, apart from the security of knowing they are backed by the federal government. Still, a negative return is a terrible price to pay for that security. Meanwhile, as the inflation rate continues to pick up, real returns from even long-term bonds could move further into negative territory. Even if your goal is strictly security of capital, you need a better asset than bonds or U.S. dollars, since neither of them will retain value.

As an investor, you must have a portfolio that can deliver strong returns over and above the inflation rate (however high it gets), and at the same time withstand deflationary episodes. Only one asset has proven itself to be an outstanding performer in both of these environments, and for this reason it should be the cornerstone of your portfolio.

The Greatest Investment to Own
During the Coming Storm

The single most essential asset to invest in for the next decade is gold. Gold has the unique ability to prosper in any type of economic turbulence, including inflation, deflation, a falling dollar, war, and even outright economic collapse. There are several reasons why.

First, we should remind you that, for reasons covered earlier, we expect the U.S. dollar will continue to lose value in coming years, while currencies of other nations, especially resource-rich nations such as Canada and Australia, will likely benefit. This will add to inflation by making imported goods more costly. If the dollar loses its value as a reserve currency, the world's central banks may start to buy fewer dollars and instead rely more on a basket of reserve currencies and assets, including gold. Owning gold can therefore help shield your savings from the inflation that results from changing currency values.

More importantly, gold has functioned as a reliable store of value for longer than any other asset. This longevity may seem like a minor trait, especially in today's world where short-term trading is predominant. However, it is this quality that makes people turn to gold during periods of crisis and uncertainty.

In 1993, J. Richard Gott III, an astrophysicist from the Institute of Advanced Study, wrote an article in *Nature*. It was probably inspired by the fall of communism and was perhaps meant as a warning that we should not be complacent about the success of Western civilization. The main tenet of the piece was that the longer something has been around, the longer it is likely to stay around. For example, a tree that has survived for more than a hundred years is considerably more likely to survive another hundred years than one that is just a few years old. Most trees do not live to be a hundred, so the few that do generally have a real advantage over their peers that will continue to help them survive. In light of this, the demise of communism was not that surprising. Communism was a relatively new system of government, and new systems are far more likely to fail than those which have withstood the test of time. (Though Gott did not say so in so many words, we must consider that the Western system of capitalism and democracy has not been around too long, either, compared to, for instance, the Roman Empire, which lasted a thousand years.)

When it comes to investing, there have been many types of currencies and assets created throughout history, most of which eventually collapsed. Two spectacular examples are tulip bulbs, which enjoyed fleeting status as financial assets in Holland during the 1630s, and the German mark, which was destroyed by hyperinflation during the early 1920s.

According to Gott's formula, however, gold is more than ten times more likely to remain a viable financial asset than the U.S. dollar. The dollar, after all, has only been around for a couple of centuries. Gold, on the other hand, has functioned as a reliable store of value for roughly six thousand years, and has been a currency for much of that time. Gold has withstood revolutions, wars, and the births and deaths of many religions and empires. Today, gold is still held as a reserve asset by many central banks. It remains a traditional savings vehicle for individuals throughout much of the world and especially in the developing nations of China and India.

Moreover, a gold coin has the unique ability to retain value despite the downfall of the government that minted it. That makes gold very different from stocks, bonds, and currencies, whose value depends on the financial health of their issuers. It is this fact that makes gold the most likely asset to survive an absolute disaster.

However, gold is more than just a tool for protecting your savings from economic turbulence. It can also help you grow considerably wealthier during such times. Gold is the one asset that can produce strong investment gains during both inflationary and deflationary periods, and that makes it an ideal asset to acquire today.

Gold's long-term price chart proves the point. From the end of 1929 to early in 2008, gold prices climbed from $20 an ounce to above $1,000, or at an annualized rate of 5 percent. During the same period, inflation (as measured by the U.S. Consumer Price Index) rose at an annualized rate of 3.2 percent. Thus, over the

Price of Gold

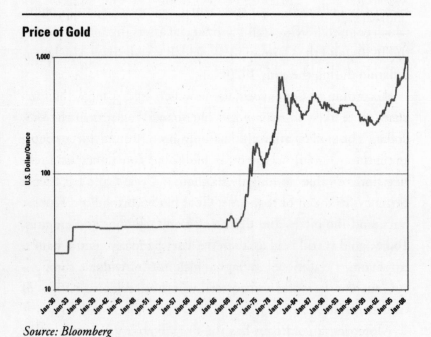

Source: Bloomberg

long term, gold has more than kept pace with inflation and served as a reliable store of value.

Let us examine these long-term results more closely. The following table tells the story. Gold's gains over the past eighty years came largely in three great bursts that together amounted to less than twenty years. The first burst occurred during the Great Depression of the 1930s, a period of deflation. The second period was the 1970s and early 1980s, when the inflation rate rose to a peacetime record high. Finally, gold has soared ever since the turn of the millennium, when the last bull market in stocks peaked.

When Gold Was Hot

Period	Years	Gold Change (Monthly Close in US$)	Real Annualized Return, %
1931–1934	2.2	20.4 to 35	29.6
1969–1980	10.2	35.1 to 680	24.4
2001–Present	7.3	250 to 1,000	18.8

Source: Bloomberg

During these three turbulent periods, gold prices rose by more than 20 percent a year in real, after-inflation terms. They were spectacular performances that left every other major asset category in the dust. In the 1970s, for example, the real return on bonds was negative 3 percent a year. Consequently, the difference between buying bonds and buying gold in that period was the difference between losing 20 percent in purchasing power or gaining more than 800 percent. And this was true even though gold's massive move in the 1970s was punctuated by a 50 percent correction.

The lesson we draw from this history is that gold will likely continue rising by at least its current rate until the economic environment becomes far more benign. With the effects of the oil and commodity squeeze only beginning to be felt, you can be confident the current bull market in gold has a lot further to go. Assuming gold rises at a 22 percent annualized rate—about average for periods of economic stress—it should reach a price of $2,500 an ounce in about five years. Moreover, that estimate could prove quite conservative if we are right in thinking that the coming years will be more turbulent than any previous ones.

In fact, if we look at the relationship between gold and other commodities, we can easily make a case for even higher gold prices. For example, historically, gold trades at about an 18 to 1 ratio to oil. However, when inflation is relatively low, the ratio between gold and oil prices tends to drop as well. In the early 1970s, the gold-oil ratio had declined to roughly 10 to 1. However, once oil and other commodities started to drive inflation higher, the ratio spiked. Between 1976 and 1981, as inflation reached double-digit heights, the gold-oil ratio surged to 20 to 1. At the same time, gold prices climbed eightfold.

As we write this, the gold-oil ratio is well below 10 to 1. If oil prices reach $200 a barrel, which we expect will happen soon, a 10 to 1 ratio would result in a gold price of $2,000 an ounce. However, as in the example of the 1970s, when inflation is very high, gold can easily overshoot the historical average. If the ratio hits the 20 to 1 level once again, that would imply a gold price of $4,000 an ounce. If oil surpasses $200 a barrel, or the ratio spikes even higher, both of which are real possibilities, gold prices could soar considerably higher. Note, too, that even at $4,000, gold would be less than five times higher than its previous $850 high in 1980, whereas the Dow is currently fifteen times higher than when gold made its previous high. Again, this implies that considerable profits for gold investors are possible.

Any way we look at it, the bull market in gold is likely to be one of the most dynamic bull markets ever witnessed in any financial asset. Gold is almost sure to be your best hope for getting through what promises to be the most turbulent economic period our civilization has ever faced. Moreover, even if the worst possible disaster befalls civilization, history shows us gold will still be prized, whereas the primary value of paper currencies may be as an energy source in your fireplace.

Of course, we do not expect gold to go straight up, any more than stocks do. Corrections, sometimes sharp ones, will occur. Indeed, gold's first run at the $1,000 level in March of 2008 was followed by a 20 percent pullback. Quite possibly, even more severe pullbacks lie ahead. *However, as long as the economy remains on a razor's edge between soaring inflation and the threat of a self-feeding decline, gold will rebound and move higher.*

The Best Ways to Invest in Gold

Purchasing gold coins or bullion and storing them in your own safe-deposit box or vault may give you the satisfaction of being able to see and touch your assets. However, it is not terribly convenient, particularly when you want to sell. Fortunately, it is now possible to invest in gold by purchasing shares in exchange-traded funds (ETFs) such as the SPDR Gold Shares (symbol: GLD). GLD holds gold bullion as its sole asset, so its share price closely tracks the price of gold. The fund gives you the ability to benefit from rising gold prices without having to store the metal yourself. GLD shares trade just like stocks, so you can hold them in a brokerage account and buy or sell them anytime during market hours.

However, we should note that during deflationary periods, gold stocks can outperform the metal itself, as mining costs will decline relative to the price of gold. In inflationary times, if gold is rising faster than other commodities, gold stocks still may have an advantage over the metal because the price of gold may grow faster than the cost of the resources used in mining, but the advantage will be relatively minor and will depend upon production profiles.

When it comes to investing in shares of gold producers, you have a great many options to choose from. The simplest method would be to invest in another exchange-traded fund, the Market Vectors Gold Miners ETF (symbol: GDX). This fund invests in all the gold and silver mining stocks that make up the AMEX Gold Miners Index, and in the same proportion. It should produce similar returns, less fees and expenses. An alternative would be to invest in a mutual fund that specializes in gold stocks, such as the Fidelity Select Gold Fund (FSAGX). This fund also gives you a diversified play on the entire gold industry, including mostly large caps, but also a small percentage of small and micro cap stocks. Another good choice is the Tocqueville Gold Fund (TGLDX), which typically focuses more heavily on small and mid cap gold stocks that are good takeover candidates in a period of rising gold prices.

If you prefer to buy shares in individual gold companies, you will need to be selective. Barrick Gold (symbol: ABX) is certainly the miner to buy if you want a stock that will follow gold and actually outperform the metal if, as we expect, gold outperforms most other commodities. The company is the world's largest gold miner and arguably the best managed among the major producers. It has many gold projects under way in various nations, making it less risky than junior explorers or single-mine companies.

The one challenge a major producer like Barrick faces is how to add significantly to its reserves and increase production. However, this company has several projects under way that could bear such fruit over the next few years. Three such projects, located in Nevada, the Dominican Republic, and Peru, could potentially boost production by nearly 30 percent in the first few years of the next decade. Barrick may also increase its gold output through acquisitions.

The company has the best balance sheet in the industry, and the best track record for exploration success. As a further plus, it is developing several platinum-related projects. Barrick's earnings will likely follow the price of gold higher until 2010, at which point its profits should start to climb faster than bullion as production increases. It is the first choice for conservative investors.

Among midsize gold miners, both Agnico-Eagle and Kinross Gold stand out, thanks to their exceptional management, financial strength, and prospects for sharp increases in gold production. Bear in mind that, even if gold prices suffer a temporary setback, low-cost mines that can sharply raise production will still generate rising profits.

Agnico-Eagle (symbol: AEM) is certainly the fastest-growing mid cap producer by a wide margin. Moreover, the company's mines produce valuable by-products, such as zinc, which generate revenues that lower the overall cost basis. Agnico-Eagle also gets high marks because the bulk of its assets are in politically secure areas such as North America.

Kinross Gold (symbol: KGC) has outstanding potential for creating large increases in production at relatively low costs. This makes the company somewhat less sensitive to changes in the price of gold, but it also means that earnings should grow at a fast clip even if gold prices fall. Moreover, because Kinross's properties have abundant gold reserves that can be profitably mined at higher prices, higher gold prices will significantly boost its underlying asset values.

We must acknowledge two factors that make Kinross a little riskier than our other picks. First, a large portion of its increased production will come from Russia. While the Russian government has sometimes treated its own companies unfairly, we do not expect it will interfere with an operation under the majority control of a foreign company. Still, the possibility cannot be ignored. Second, any company planning to bring new production online is vulnerable to execution risk. Nonetheless, we think Kinross offers good value that outweighs these risks.

Precious Alternatives

To some extent, the forces that will drive gold prices higher will do the same for other precious metals such as silver and platinum, but there are differences. Silver, for example, underperformed gold during the Great Depression, but then it outperformed it in the late 1970s and early 1980s, partly because of the Hunt brothers' attempt to corner the market on the metal. More recently, silver and gold have marched in lockstep. Platinum, meanwhile, has outperformed the other two in recent years, thanks to its scarcity and high demand as an industrial metal.

Longer term, however, the extent to which a commodity is used in manufacturing products makes it less attractive as a store of value. In fact, one of gold's prime virtues as an investment is that there are not many industrial uses for the metal.

We can assume that the investment value of any metal is composed of two main factors: its ability to serve as a store of value and its usefulness as a raw material in industrial applications. Gold is the best store of value in part because it does not oxidize. It will not tarnish, rust, or otherwise become degraded over time. This makes it superior to other metals such as iron, copper, or silver.

As for a metal's industrial applications, these add volatility to prices, which may produce higher returns under the right conditions but is not a desirable feature in an asset intended to preserve value. For instance, when economic growth is taking place, demand for raw materials increases, which drives up the prices of industrial metals. Inflation is largely a result of rising commodity prices, which makes commodities a good hedge against inflation. However, during a bout of recession and deflation, demand for commodities falls. To whatever extent a precious metal is also an industrial commodity, you can expect its price to be negatively impacted. (This is why silver prices fell during the Depression.) For this reason, metals such as silver and platinum are not useful hedges against deflation. Only gold can fulfill this role since, with few industrial uses, its price is based almost entirely on its ability to store value.

Nonetheless, as inflation rises, investors can expect to reap excellent returns from silver and platinum. Platinum is a rare metal that is in strong demand for use in making catalytic converters for diesel engines and in hydrogen fuel cells. Silver, too, is enjoying an increased number of industrial uses while above-ground stockpiles of the metal have been depleted to historically low levels.

As with gold, you can buy silver and platinum coins and bullion as investments, if you do not mind the inconvenience and cost of storage. There is no platinum exchange-traded fund at the moment, but there is one that invests in silver, the iShares Silver Trust (symbol: SLV). As with GLD, SLV trades on the stock exchange like any common share and gives you an easy way to invest in the metal.

As for stocks, the world's largest silver mining company is Pan American Silver (symbol: PAAS). The company has a multibillion dollar market cap and minimal debt. It has managed to increase its silver production every year since 1995. Returns on investment have historically been excellent. Worth noting, too, is that Bill Gates, and the company's chairman, Ross Beaty, are both major shareholders. With ongoing and newly developing operations in

Peru, Argentina, Mexico, and Bolivia, the company expects to be producing 25 million ounces of silver annually by 2009.

Most of the platinum group metals (PGMs)—which include rhodium, iridium, osmium, ruthenium, and palladium, as well as platinum itself—are mined in the Bushveld Igneous Complex in South Africa. The world's largest platinum producer, which operates in this region, is Anglo Platinum (symbol: AGPPY). In 2007, it produced over 2.4 million ounces of platinum, in addition to smaller amounts of gold, nickel, copper, and other PGMs. Our other favorite South African platinum miner is Impala Platinum (symbol: IMPUY). While this company currently produces less platinum than Anglo, it has plans to rapidly increase production over the next few years.

Investing in precious metals will give you an excellent way to make strong returns over and above the inflation rate as the commodity crisis pushes the world closer to Game Over. They should be a core holding in your portfolio.

However, in addition to precious metals, several other investment categories also exhibit strong potential for profits in an inflationary environment. We review these in the next chapter.

CHAPTER 15

BRAC: Staying Afloat by Investing Abroad

As we've stressed, because of its unique ability to thrive under any kind of economic turbulence, gold is the single most important investment to own in coming years. In periods of recession or deflation, it will keep you afloat even as nearly all other investments crash and burn. At the same time, during the longer stretches of steep inflation that we expect, the gains in gold should easily outpace rising prices.

Still, during those times when inflation, spurred in part by the growing scarcity of commodities, has the upper hand, it will also pay to have a stake in companies that control the remaining supplies of commodities. Below we look at some of these other attractive investments that should more than hold their own against inflation and that will nicely complement your position in gold.

From BRIC to BRAC (and Someday BRAAC)

Imagine for a moment that just one country contained the vast bulk of one essential mineral. As other countries used up their own far more limited reserves, the price of this mineral would rise dramatically. In addition, the currency of the country blessed with the lion's share of that mineral would also gain in value, simply because every other nation would need that currency in order to buy the mineral. As supplies of many commodities begin to run out, we can similarly expect that resource-rich nations will see their currencies gain value against those of resource-poor nations, such as the United States and European countries.

Many economists today refer to the four fastest-growing developing nations by the acronym BRIC, which stands for Brazil, Russia, India, and China. Investing in the BRIC nations has certainly been a way to profit from growth. *However, we believe the biggest gains in coming years will be made by those who invest in the four nations endowed with the most surplus natural resources.* These are the BRAC nations: Brazil, Russia, Australia, and Canada. All four are net exporters of fuels and other natural products. They will certainly lead the pack in a world where resource shortages are worsening.

Of course, China and India will remain the largest and fastest-growing emerging economies, and their future on the world stage is bright. However, the major advantage Chindia has at the moment is cheap labor, but that advantage will not last. Wages in China and India are beginning to rise and will continue to do so as their economies expand and living standards improve.

That is not to say the currencies of China and India will weaken. As we discussed earlier, a huge gap exists today between the true economic value of Chindia's GDP and its apparent value in U.S. dollars, meaning that Chindian currencies are grossly undervalued. The natural tendency is for them to gain ground against the dollar. We therefore expect Chindian currencies will more than hold their own as resource prices rise, creating higher inflation and knocking the legs out from under the dollar.

However, as growing consumption in Asia and the rest of the world pushes demand for commodities higher, it is the currencies of Australia and Canada that will experience the biggest gains. One cannot overstate how important relative resource independence is in a world where resources are becoming ever scarcer and more expensive. Australia and Canada, along with the other BRAC nations, will enjoy lower and more predictable costs, which will translate into stronger growth, lower inflation, and rising currency values. In fact, this is happening already. Less than ten years ago, the Canadian dollar (nicknamed the "loonie" after the loon that appears on the Canadian one-dollar coin) traded at around $0.65 US. Today it has risen to near parity. Other BRAC currencies have seen strong gains as well.

Naturally, many other factors, including monetary and fiscal policies as well as politics, affect the relative performance of a currency. However, greater resource independence gives BRAC nations greater freedom to chart their economic course. The recent uptrends in BRAC currencies and stock markets, as opposed to

U.S. Dollar Index

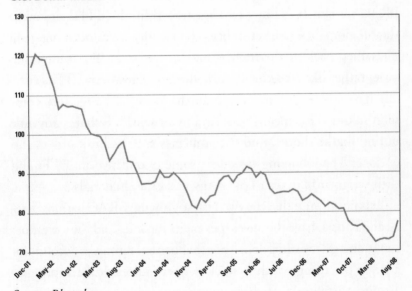

Source: Bloomberg

BRAC Currencies

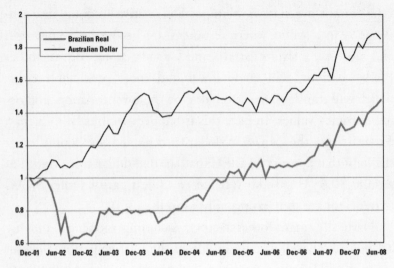

Source: Bloomberg

the downtrend in the U.S. dollar, are evidence that such increased leeway does translate into positive results.

The easiest way for investors to gain a broad stake in the BRAC nations is to buy exchange-traded funds (ETFs) linked to their major stock market indices. ETFs offer investors a one-stop diversified play on a particular nation, sector, index, or investing style, rather like traditional mutual funds. However, ETFs generally have lower fees and trade on the stock exchange like common shares. This means you can buy or sell ETF shares anytime during market hours, and use strategies such as limit orders and options. The following table lists some of our favorite ETFs and their weightings in terms of energy and other materials.

It is no surprise that the two fastest-growing BRAC nations, Brazil and Russia, have the lowest per capita incomes and the lowest per capita energy consumption—nor that natural resources account for a larger percentage of their stock market indices. It is tempting to assume, therefore, that these two nations have the most potential.

4 Nations, 4 Compelling ETFs

Country	Brazil	Russia	Australia	Canada
ETF Symbol	EWZ	RSX	EWA	EWC
Sector Weight in ETF (%)				
Materials	33	25	28	12
Energy	24	43	9	24
Other	43	32	63	64
P/E	21.9	18.2	18.7	23.1
GDP per Capita (in US$)	4,044	2,620	23,262	25,894
Energy Use per Capita*	1,122	4,517	5,978	8,417
Per Capita Growth (%)	2.4	7.2	1.0	1.7

*Kilograms of oil equivalent
Sources: Bloomberg, World Bank

However, that is true only to a certain point. As their economies develop, Brazil and Russia will increasingly need to draw on their own abundant resources for internal consumption to fuel their own growth. By contrast, Australia and Canada have higher incomes and more mature, service-oriented economies. They are less reliant on their own natural resources. Consequently, they will be able to conserve resources as they grow, leaving more available for export.

As is typical when it comes to investing, one must balance potential risk and reward. The rich resource bases of all four nations give them an advantage in sustaining growth and strengthening their currencies. However, Brazil and Russia offer stronger growth with greater risk, while the developed status of Australia and Canada makes those nations a safer haven in a commodity-short world. An investor should allocate capital among the BRAC nations according to his or her risk tolerance.

We should also point out that, as a result of the bull market in commodities, investors are beginning to get excited about opportunities in Africa, a continent long viewed as economically dormant or regressing but that has an abundance of undeveloped resources. Economic growth in the region has recently accelerated to record highs, with sub-Saharan Africa averaging better than 5 percent GDP growth since 2001. Investors currently have fewer options for investing in Africa than in the BRAC nations; however, there are some African resource producers we view quite favorably, including, as mentioned before, the African platinum miners Impala and Anglo Platinum. It may not be long until the financial world adds an *A* for Africa to our acronym, in recognition of the importance of investing in BRAAC.

The World's Best Resource Stocks

Another way to capitalize on soaring commodity prices is to buy shares in individual resource-producing companies. Many of the world's largest and best-run miners, for instance, operate in a number of nations, including the BRAC countries, and produce many different commodities, thus providing investors with diversification outside the U.S. dollar, as well as exposure to the commodities boom.

For example, the company that offers arguably the best exposure to the entire resource sector is Australia-based BHP Billiton (symbol: BHP). This exceptionally well-managed behemoth is the largest diversified commodities firm in the world. It provides investors with a stake in virtually every major industrial commodity, including oil. In addition, the company operates in nearly every significant commodity-producing country.

Another well-diversified miner is Rio Tinto (symbol: RTP). This company has a slightly greater stake in steel and uranium, while BHP Billiton provides more exposure to energy and base metals. We should note that, in November of 2007, BHP Billiton launched a hostile takeover bid for Rio Tinto which, if successful, would certainly add to Billiton's resource base. As the commodity squeeze worsens, and unless exploration becomes more fruitful, we expect large companies will increasingly use acquisitions to add to their production. Regardless of the outcome of Billiton's bid, both these companies are extremely profitable and should reward investors handsomely as the commodity squeeze intensifies.

We should also mention Southern Copper (symbol: PCU), another potential winner and a nearly pure play on copper, one of the most commonly used metals in construction. Due to extensive new construction in China and elsewhere in recent years, copper inventories have fallen and prices have risen substantially. This trend will likely accelerate if, as we expect, the building of a new alternative energy infrastructure commences in the next few years.

Copper: Price vs. Supply

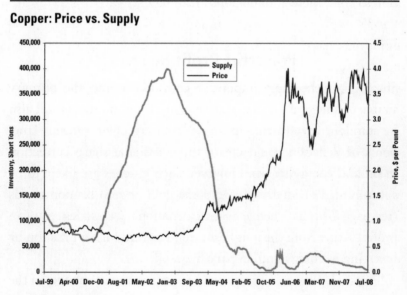

Source: Bloomberg

While we take pains here to describe some of the better commodity investments, as seen at this time, we must point out that many commodity producers will do well in the months and years ahead. As long as worldwide growth remains strong, the economy will maintain an inflationary bias and commodity prices will keep rising. Producers with good balance sheets that are positioned to increase their production as well as benefit from higher prices should reward investors handsomely.

We should also point out that, while we expect the recommendations in these pages will be valid for some time, new investment opportunities arise quite frequently. Since you are reading this book some months after it was written, we may have already revised our opinions on the most promising stocks. You can find our up-to-date thinking on the markets and on individual stocks in the monthly investment newsletter, *The Complete Investor*, information on which may be found at www.completeinvestor.com.

Of course, if you were to choose just one commodity in addition to gold, there is an obvious candidate.

Powerful Profit Sources

Since oil is the most important commodity and the primary source of energy used to maintain civilization, oil stocks will also be standout investments in an inflationary environment. True, bouts of deflation could create the occasional sharp correction in oil and energy stocks. However, such glitches are likely to be short-lived. Provided you own some gold or zero coupon bonds (see page 204) as a hedge against deflationary episodes, you can profit further from the long-term trend toward higher inflation by investing in energy and, in particular, oil.

Again, however, it is important to stay on top of changes in the market and to base your investment decisions on current information. For instance, the past few years, leadership among oil stocks has changed. In the early 2000s, it was the major oil producers that made the biggest gains. At that time, the high yields and relative safety of the majors appealed to investors seeking insurance, much the same way bonds did. However, rising inflation will make these so-called safe securities less safe going forward.

We have already pointed out that one of the problems facing major oil firms is their growing inability to increase production. Yet, as oil supplies fall behind demand, raising production will become top priority, and companies that can assist in this area will benefit the most. As the following table shows, in the 1970s, the last time oil supplies tightened, most oil companies delivered above-average investment returns. However, the bulk of the profits were not generated by the major oil producers but by the oil service companies. The reason is that, unlike the majors, oil service companies are not involved in the production, transportation, or marketing of oil and other fuels. Instead, they are contracted by major oil companies and the companies that explore for oil and natural gas to primarily do the work of constructing, drilling, and servicing new oil wells and fields. Because of this, their business is more cyclical in nature, thriving when the supply-demand pressure on oil tightens and waning when supplies outstrip demand.

As oil fell from its highs in the 1980s, many long-term oil projects were put on hold because they were uneconomical at lower prices. But in coming years, as oil prices continue to rise, companies will want to restart many of these projects, which will create more need for oil services. Oil service companies have an additional advantage in today's world because, as oil becomes harder to find and extract, oil producers will rely on oil service companies for their technological assistance. Oil service companies will therefore reap the benefits of the growing scarcity of oil while incurring few of the costs. Consequently, we expect that within the energy

Returns from Oil Investments During the 1970s

Investment	Avg. annual nominal return (%)	Avg. annual real return (%)	Total real return (%)
Crude Oil	26.4	19	469.5
Big Oil Companies	14.2	6.8	93.1
Independent Oil Producers	19.2	11.8	205.1
Oil Service Companies	31	23.6	732.1

Source: The Complete Investor *(Stephen Leeb, editor)*

sector, the oil service companies will once again be the growth leaders as well as the companies most likely to outpace inflation. Within this group, the most notable firms are Schlumberger (symbol: SLB), Nabors (symbol: NBR), Transocean (symbol: RIG), Baker Hughes (symbol: BHI), National Oilwell Varco (symbol: NOV), and Halliburton (symbol: HAL). Each of these companies offers above-average growth along with an exceptionally low valuation. Indeed, as we write this, many oil drillers and service stocks are priced as though oil were still selling for under $80. When oil nears the $200 mark, these stocks will have some rapid catching up to do, which will translate into very high returns for investors.

Among the oil service stocks, Schlumberger certainly stands out. The company plays a prominent role in every major oil project in the world, offering a wide variety of drilling, well construction, information technology, seismic imaging, and maintenance services to the oil and gas industry. Barring a severe worldwide recession (which could only delay, not halt, the frantic search for more oil), this broad-based technological leader is set to grow by more than 20 percent annually for years to come. Its franchise is so strong that the company cannot only pass along higher costs, it can pass them along with price increases to spare, as shown by its soaring profitability. Amazingly, Schlumberger has been selling at close to all-time low valuations in recent years, a remarkable disconnect that will likely correct in the near future.

For further diversification among the BRAC nations, investors might consider energy-related companies such as the Canadian Oil Sands Trust (COSWF). This investment trust is a significant minor owner of a major project in Canada's tar sands, one of the few oil regions where production can be significantly increased. Consequently, the Canadian Oil Sands Trust is one of the few oil production beneficiaries likely to exhibit a rising stream of income independent of oil prices. The company currently operates as an income trust under Canadian law. Because its income is essentially passive, and because of the specifics of Canada's current income code, the company can, at present, pass along all its receipts to investors in the form of a distribution. Consequently, it offers a very high yield.

It is important to note that the Canadian government has planned changes to the tax code that will impose a 25 percent tax on distributions from income trusts, starting in 2011. These changes will likely affect Canadian Oil Sands' cash from operating activities and, therefore, future distributions. Nonetheless, it is the company's stake in the Canadian tar sands that makes it an appealing investment, not its structure, and investor returns should continue to grow as the Canadian dollar appreciates and more oil is produced from the tar sands.

Another promising choice is the Russian firm Gazprom, which has a near monopoly on the production, distribution, and export of Russian natural gas. It also produces oil. Gazprom is arguably the most powerful company in the world, thanks to its enormous control over European gas supplies and prices. With a large inventory of undeveloped properties and the prospect of additional licenses, the company should be able to increase production for the foreseeable future. Of course, as we mentioned before, Russia is a more risky nation to invest in. Nonetheless, this company's tremendous upside potential justifies holding a small position in its stock. (While the company does not trade on U.S. exchanges, investors can purchase American Depository Receipts [ADRs] for Gazprom shares, which trade on the pink sheets under the symbol OGZPY.)

Though not a BRAC play, the oil producer XTO Energy (symbol: XTO) may also be a good bet. This small domestic oil company controls a hefty portion of the remaining untapped oil in the United States. We expect that these strong assets will contribute to growth for this company in the years to come.

With energy prices rising, many nations plan to bring new nuclear power plants online to reduce their dependence on fossil fuels. As of December 2007, thirty-five new nuclear plants were under construction around the world, according to the International Atomic Energy Agency. As these begin producing electricity, uranium prices will likely rise rapidly. Two stocks that should profit from this event are the Australian uranium miner Energy Resources (symbol: EGRAF) and Cameco (symbol: CCJ). Energy Resources is poised to become not only the fastest-growing uranium producer but also one of the fastest growing of all commodity companies. On the other hand, Cameco, a Canadian firm, is the world's largest uranium producer. It has suffered in recent months due to unfortunate (and, we suspect, temporary) problems. However, as these problems are dealt with and uranium prices rise, Cameco shares should also do well.

The "Defensive" Plays to Avoid

Just as commodities and investments leveraged to commodities will thrive in the prevailing inflationary environment for the next decade or longer, other sectors will severely underperform.

Moreover, because rising inflation tends to invert the usual rules of investing, many of the worst performers will be those that are normally considered safe havens.

For instance, stocks in the household goods and personal care sectors are generally considered to be defensive investments. Because they provide products and services for which demand remains steady under all conditions, they are less susceptible to economic slowdowns than other sectors. Consequently, investors are usually willing to pay a higher price for the earnings of these companies, with the result that they tend to have high P/E ratios. (Traditionally, a P/E of 20 or more is considered high. At that level, an investor would be paying $20 for every $1 of a company's earnings. On the other hand, a P/E under 10 is considered low.)

The problem is that, during periods of high inflation, stocks with high P/E ratios tend to see those ratios shrink. There are several reasons for this. First, inflation creates uncertainty regarding future profits, which makes investors reluctant to pay a high price for a company's earnings. Another reason is that a company's earnings growth is generally made up of two parts: business expansion and its ability to raise prices (pass inflation on to its customers). Inflationary growth is not considered as valuable as growth that comes from business expansion, since it typically applies to all companies and cannot be used to identify the best management. Consequently,

Returns from "Defensive" Sectors

Defensive Sectors	Nominal Changes: 1970 High to 1979 Low
Beverages	–13.00%
Cosmetics	–45.60%
Retail Stores	–34.00%

Source: The Complete Investor

when inflationary growth makes up a large part of profit growth, investors will not value earnings as highly, so P/E ratios decline. This process limits returns from high P/E stocks. As you can see from the table on page 201, between 1970 and 1979, when inflation reached double digits, defensive stocks delivered negative real returns.

As the current inflationary wave unfolds, investors will do better if they stick with companies that feature both strong growth and low P/Es (such as the oil service stocks mentioned above). The so-called "defensive" stocks will stop being defensive as soon as inflation takes hold. Many others with high P/E ratios not supported by strong growth, including many technology stocks, will likely be among the biggest losers.

Also to be avoided is any sector where costs and profits are strongly and negatively leveraged to the prices of commodities, especially oil. These include such sectors as chemicals, automobiles, and airlines. Naturally, rising fuel prices cut deeply into the profitability of airlines. Chemical producers are similarly affected because oil is an important raw material for them. Among automakers, the impact of higher fuel prices is felt more by companies that manufacture vehicles with higher fuel consumption, such as SUVs. These suffer from declining sales as gasoline prices rise. Nonetheless, all automakers will suffer as rising fuel costs encourage families to cut back on the number of vehicles they own and

Returns from Sectors Adversely Leveraged to Rising Oil

Sectors Adversely Leveraged to Rising Oil Prices	Nominal Changes: 1970 High to 1979 Low
Airlines	−37.00%
Autos	−55.00%
Chemicals	−47.30%

Source: The Complete Investor

rely more on public transit or carpooling. As the table shows, all three of these sectors produced horrendous investment returns in the 1970s, and we think they are set to repeat that performance.

Defensive Investments Worth Owning

Two investments will offer genuine defensive benefits during the next ten years. The first is Berkshire Hathaway (symbol: BRK/B), run by Warren Buffett, who is arguably the greatest investor alive today. Berkshire is one of the most complex and widely diversified conglomerates in the world, with stakes in companies ranging from furniture makers to energy utilities. It is also a holding company for a range of publicly traded stocks. Yet, despite such a diverse mix, Berkshire is the dominant company in its main business, reinsurance, where it maintains an enormous advantage over all rivals.

Reinsurance, the underwriting of primary insurers, is a rapidly growing industry. An unhappy combination of weather-related disasters and urbanization has vastly increased the number and costs of both natural and unnatural disasters, spurring the need for insurers and reinsurers alike. Berkshire leads the pack because its capital base—which determines how much insurance a company can write—is about three times larger than that of its nearest rival's. The company's insurance subsidiaries enjoy a triple A rating from Standard and Poor's, and its financial strength virtually ensures it will enjoy long-term growth in at least the low to midteens, even if, as we expect, most reinsurers and other financial stocks perform poorly in the coming years. In fact, the only scenario we can imagine in which Berkshire could fail to deliver is if Buffett retires and is replaced by an incompetent successor. However, since that is highly unlikely, Berkshire remains a great defensive, all-weather holding.

Finally, in addition to gold, there is one other investment category that offers a hedge against a possible bout of deflation, and that is zero coupon bonds. Zero coupon bonds differ from regular bonds in that they pay no interest. Instead, investors buy them at a steep discount to their face value and collect the full face value when they mature. Your return is the difference between the two prices.

The reason zero coupon bonds are a hedge against deflation derives from the fact that bond yields and bond prices are like two ends of a teeter-totter. When one rises, the other falls, and vice versa. During deflationary periods, interest rates and bond yields fall while bond prices rise. Because the implied yield on a zero coupon bond derives entirely from its discount, it is more sensitive to interest rate changes and its price will rise more than other bonds, helping to compensate the buyer for any losses on other investments. The longer the maturity of the zero coupon bond, the greater the price appreciation. This is why, for maximum protection against deflation, investors should own the longest-dated zeroes available.

Zero coupon bonds are created through a U.S. Treasury program called STRIPS (Separate Trading of Registered Interest and Principal of Securities). While Treasury securities are never issued as zero coupon bonds, each interest payment (coupon) for a given bond can be separated from the principal. The coupons and principal can then trade independently as zero coupon securities. You can buy and hold STRIPS through financial institutions and government securities brokers and dealers.

Alternatively, you can put money into a mutual fund that invests primarily in zero coupon bonds, such as the American Century zero coupon bond funds, which are easy to buy or sell even through discount or online brokers.

CHAPTER 16

Investing in the New
Resource War

As the global competition for commodities intensifies, nations and even regional separatist groups will increasingly resort to violence and military action to protect their natural resources, or to steal the resources of others. The United States will therefore need to beef up military spending in the years ahead, making defense a sector that will provide strong investor returns. This point was driven home by the Russian invasion of Georgia in August of 2008.

At first glance, the event may have looked like the resurgence of last century's Cold War. Two tiny regions within Georgia, South Ossetia and Abkhazia, had declared independence from the rest of the country years before. Though nominally parts of Georgia, they had aligned themselves with Russia, to the extent that residents of both regions traveled on Russian passports. Georgia, on the other hand, had allied itself more strongly with the West. The United States helped train the Georgian army and sponsored the nation's membership application to NATO, despite Russia's objections.

Georgia wanted to promote stability by bringing its breakaway regions back under its authority. Such a move would have improved its chances of being accepted into NATO. Russia, which has resisted the spread of NATO eastward, used the excuse of protecting its citizens in South Ossetia to assert control over all of Georgia.

Certainly the story has all the hallmarks of a Cold War saga. However, this is not 1960. The Russian invasion of Georgia may have less to do with a struggle between communism and capitalism and more to do with competition over energy supplies.

Georgia, while not particularly resource rich, is home to the Baku-Tbilisi-Ceyhan (BTC) pipeline that carries oil from Azerbaijan and the Caspian Sea to Western markets. This pipeline was specifically built to bypass Russia and let the oil flow through pro-Western territory. However, realizing that energy is the major source of power in the world today, Russia is determined to control as much as it can. We noted earlier that the Russian natural gas producer Gazprom plays an extremely important role in the world. The gas it sends to Western Europe is essential for that region's survival. The amount of oil that flows through Georgia via the BTC pipeline equals the world's current excess capacity—estimated at about 1.5 million barrels, circa 2008. With de facto control of that pipeline, Russia will utterly dominate energy supplies to Europe, and ultimately the United States as well. We have no doubt that was Russia's real purpose in sending its army into Georgia. An additional benefit of the invasion is that from now on other nations will think twice about building pipelines that bypass Russian control. *In short, we are now witnessing not a Cold War but a Resource War.*

Sadly, the United States can only do so much to defend our interests in Russia's backyard. Certainly, we could threaten to go to war in defense of Georgia. However, Russia is no puny Middle East regime. The country has a sizable military and a plentiful supply of weapons, including nuclear and other weapons of mass destruction. During the Cold War, peace was maintained between the West and the East through the principle of Mutual Assured Destruction, or MAD. Under MAD, any nuclear attack launched from one side would be met with an equal or greater response by the other. The result would be the total destruction of both sides, and quite possibly life on this planet. When it comes to any conflict between the U.S. and Russia today, MAD still applies. Open war is unthinkable.

As for a smaller conflict using conventional weapons in Eastern Europe, Russia would have a big edge because of its proximity to Georgia and other members of the former Soviet Union (FSU). We mention these ex-Soviet nations because we cannot rule out the possibility that Russia might seize the opportunity to reannex any of its former allies that currently have access to the oil reserves on the Caspian Sea.

Nor can we win a Resource War with Russia the way we won the Cold War. In the 1980s, the United States held a decisive advantage over the former Soviet Union. Our economy was stronger and we could afford to outspend our rivals when it came to defense. Over time, Russia could not match the American military budget, and its economy collapsed in the attempt. The Russian economy remained in shambles throughout much of the 1990s. Living conditions deteriorated so much, in fact, Russia was lucky it didn't experience a new revolution. As it was, the Soviet Union broke apart and life expectancy in the former member states fell rapidly. Economic growth turned negative.

But Russia's star has risen in recent years as resources have become a more critical part of the global equation. The ascent of Chindia and the rest of the developing world, along with the spread of capitalism, has strengthened worldwide economic growth. And with more growth, resources have become utterly essential. We have already discussed why growth in the developing world will remain strong and put increasing pressure on the world's commodity supplies.

In a world where resources rule, the United States can no longer bury Russia economically. The simple truth of the matter is that the U.S. has far fewer surplus natural resources than Russia and is forced to purchase more commodities from other nations. Russia, being resource rich, is therefore in the stronger position. This is not a pleasant reality to be faced with, but it's unavoidable.

Our quandary goes well beyond Russia. Even though China is also dependent on others for natural resources, it, too, has a distinct advantage over the United States. As an economy in which the government plays a very active role, China is much better positioned to explore for resources in the more dangerous parts of the world where they may be located. For example, if an American company wants to explore for oil in the war-torn country of Nigeria or other African countries where the local government cannot provide adequate protection for foreign or even national workers, it has to bring its own police force. It has to bear the costs of training such a private army, as well as paying for their food, housing, and transportation. Measured in energy, the costs are tremendous and often prohibitive for a private company operating in an unstable region. It can take more energy than the company could produce.

On the other hand, a company such as PetroChina, which is controlled by the Chinese government, can count on the support of China's massive standing military force. It can gather whatever military personnel it needs to explore for and produce oil in even the most dangerous places in the world. Naturally, the same applies to Chinese companies producing other resources as well.

Of course, in a full-fledged global Resource War, no one will win. Such a war could easily consume as many resources as can be won through combat. Unfortunately, history is filled with examples of nations using violence to secure resources. The Russian incursion into the Caucasus is only the latest example. Some argue that the U.S. invasion of Iraq was also partly driven by the desire to secure oil supplies. No one would argue that Saddam Hussein was not an evil dictator, but there were other unmitigated villains in the world at the time the United States invaded Iraq. Why didn't we overthrow, for example, Robert Mugabe as well? Our point is that, rather than allow wasteful wars to erupt, it would be better if an international agreement could be reached that will allow for peaceful rationing of the world's remaining resource deposits. It would be in everyone's interests. After all, even the resource-rich countries will eventually run out of vital materials.

Until such an agreement can be made, the only weapon the United States has with which to defend its interests and even out the playing field with Russia and China is an overwhelming edge in defense capability. While the U.S. and Russia (and to some extent China) have considerable nuclear arsenals, America still has the largest military in the world. In any conflict involving strictly conventional weapons, we are much more than a match for either of these two powers. The U.S. government's challenge going forward is to make sure we maintain that military superiority. The task won't be easy. Both the Russians, because of their edge in resources, and the Chinese, because of their edge in labor costs, can also afford major defense expenditures. Despite our deficits we will have to keep up and then some. With our conventional forces and our technological edge, we must promote political stability and safeguard our access to resources around the world, especially in the Middle East, South America, and parts of Africa where essential mineral deposits lie. America's military, for example, is critical to our relationship with Saudi Arabia and

Defense Spending as Percentage of GDP

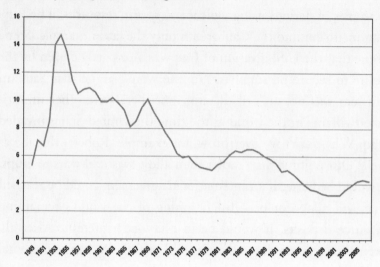

Source: www.cbo.gov

arguably our only hope for keeping Iran from expanding its influence over Iraq.

Ghoulish as it seems, this new arms race is good news for defense stocks.

Currently, the United States outspends all other countries on defense. Yet defense spending amounts to only 4 percent of GDP, which is low by historical standards. During the Korean War, America spent 12 percent of its GDP on defense. Even in the 1980s, defense spending was 6 percent of GDP. Many of the U.S. military's major conventional warfare systems are aging, the result of the slowdown in new procurement following the fall of the Soviet Union. Consequently, most experts expect the Pentagon will start ordering new generations of tanks, planes, and ships in coming years, probably after the Iraq conflict subsides. And future presidents will surely feel compelled to raise defense spending from today's relatively low levels. All that new spending will make defense stocks excellent investments.

The defense industry in the United States is a near oligarchy comprised of a small handful of companies. The four largest—Northrop Grumman, Raytheon, General Dynamics, and Lockheed Martin—are joined by only a few smaller firms, such as L-3 Communications. Yet, as the situation in Georgia reminds us, this handful of companies will be increasingly vital to America's future. We therefore expect to see them receive substantial new government contracts over the next few years.

Even in a market that remains turbulent, the best-placed defense companies should be stalwart and fairly steady performers. *We must point out that, following 9/11, defense stocks were one of the few market groups that not only outperformed the market but posted very solid gains.* It's true that, like other manufacturers, major defense companies will face skyrocketing costs of steel and other materials as Absolute Peak Commodities approaches. However, unlike the automobile industry, for instance, they will almost surely be able to pass these costs on to the government, which would rather pay through the nose than fall behind militarily in the tumultuous period to come.

If we had to narrow down the list of defense stocks, we have two we would recommend above the rest. First, Northrop Grumman (symbol: NOC) stands out as a diversified contractor best known for shipbuilding. However, with the Pentagon ordering fewer ships over the past fifteen years, the company has beefed up its presence in faster-growing areas. Information and services currently make up a larger percentage of its revenues, followed by aerospace and electronics. Northrop's major contracts include those for Nimitz-class aircraft carriers, Virginia-class submarines, and the B2 bomber.

Our second top defense pick is Raytheon (symbol: RTN), a leader in defense, electronics, information technology systems, and missile technology. Its products have military, border security, and aerospace applications. Thanks to its technological edge, Raytheon has been one of the fastest-growing large U.S. defense contractors.

Rather than act as the prime contractor on big-ticket programs, Raytheon serves as a subcontractor. It supplies complex missile technology, systems-integration knowledge, and network-centric command and control systems that can be used in a variety of ships, planes, and other weapons projects. These specialties position the company for the fastest-growing part of the Pentagon's budget: surveillance and intelligence projects. In addition, if a national missile-defense plan moves forward, Raytheon will likely be a major player.

But if you were to choose Lockheed or General Dynamics, or even a smaller company like L-3 Communications, we don't think you can go wrong in the coming turbulent world. Defense companies also get relatively high marks for being resistant to decline during turbulent markets. They are perhaps the only industrial companies whose earnings are nearly assured no matter what happens in the market.

CHAPTER 17

Investing in the Solutions

Though it may seem hard to believe, in truth, we are basically optimists, as well as opportunists. It is our deep hope that the world will quickly rally to recognize the threat of Peak Commodities very soon and will begin the massive program needed to save our current lifestyle: a program of resource conservation, infrastructure building, and the development of alternative, and preferably renewable, energy supplies.

Such a program will likely require over a trillion dollars of government funding in the United States alone, and equally strong commitments from other nations as well. That flood of money will also be a tremendous windfall for investors in those companies that contribute to the solutions. In addition, by investing in these companies early on, you will contribute to the solution to our energy problems and help strengthen America against the coming turmoil.

Today's Pioneers

First, let us consider alternative energies. To say they are critical to our future would be a severe understatement. Yet, thanks to wide-

Historical Energy Consumption

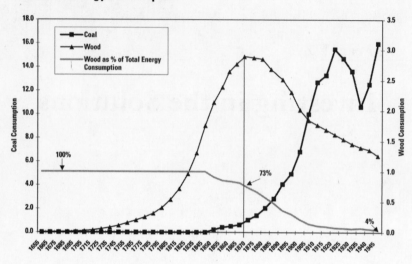

Source: Department of Energy

spread denial of the energy problem, they are woefully underdeveloped. Consider that the last time America's primary energy source peaked and we were forced to switch to another was back in the 1870s, when wood gave way to coal. As the chart above shows, by the time wood consumption peaked, coal was already providing about 35 percent of our energy needs.

Today, however, alternative energies—including nuclear—account for only about 15 percent of U.S. energy consumption. Clean, renewable energies, such as solar and wind, account for less than 1 percent. Clearly, we have a lot of catching up to do in a short space of time. We will need to make a heroic effort, and the transition period will be turbulent, but the only alternative would be to allow our entire economy and social order to collapse.

From an investment point of view, the alternative energy industry today is small, confusing, and risky. There are many tiny companies that are researching and developing alternative energy and energy-saving technologies. Predicting which among these will win significant market share, let alone profitability, is as challenging as it was to determine which small technology and Internet stocks in the late 1990s would survive and prosper for more than a decade. Many have a great story or idea but no history of producing real profits.

Investors therefore need to be cautious. Our advice is to buy the strongest players in the sector, while avoiding companies that are technology specific. The companies that are too young and reliant on a single, albeit very exciting, technology are likely to be short-lived and subject to competitive pressures from newer, better solutions. Many technologies may also find themselves defeated by the vicious circle in commodities that will drive raw material costs higher. Even the most successful, such as First Solar, which was discussed earlier, may run into resource-related roadblocks.

At present, we know of only a handful of alternative energy stocks that stand out from the herd. But before you read on, we should emphasize that these companies are the most speculative of all the investment recommendations we lay out in this book. The vicious circles in commodities and other causes of uncertainty in the years ahead make them very high risk.

In addition to Energy Resources, which we mentioned earlier, six others have particularly strong growth profiles at the moment. They are Exelon (symbol: EXC), FPL Group (symbol: FPL), Gamesa (symbol: GCTAF), Ormat Technologies (symbol: ORA), Sasol (symbol: SSL), and Vesta (symbol: VWSYF). None of these is a pie-in-the-sky, "someday" kind of enterprise. All of them currently produce energy and have significant and fast-growing revenue streams. In fact, one of the most heartening facts on the energy front is that these companies' profits should continue to burgeon.

The seven stocks cover the gamut of practical energy alternatives, including geothermal, wind, and nuclear. We have omitted biofuel stocks intentionally. For one thing, there are no dedicated, rapidly growing biofuel companies at the moment. Moreover, as we pointed out earlier, switching to biofuels—in particular, ethanol—is a disastrously misguided approach to meeting our energy needs. Not only is ethanol at least as dirty as fossil fuels, many studies suggest its production consumes more energy than it yields. Switching to ethanol fuel is simply substituting one scarce commodity, food, for another, oil.

Within our group of serious alternative energy stocks, FPL, the country's leading wind generator and a producer of nuclear energy, and Exelon, the leading nuclear generator, are perhaps the safest plays. Though their growth rates are among the lowest of the six, their defensive characteristics are compelling. If the United States or indeed the world slides into a full-fledged economic downturn, both companies should hold steady. Their plain-vanilla utility operations make them immune to even severe economic declines. At the same time, their deregulated operations—FPL's wind and nuclear businesses and the bulk of Exelon's nuclear generation—should experience unfettered growth, resulting in accelerated growth overall. In fact, growth for both companies could rise dramatically since, over the intermediate term, nuclear energy will likely become an increasingly important alternative to fossil fuels. Exelon, the largest and most skilled nuclear operator, and FPL should both be on the very short list of companies granted licenses for new nuclear plants.

Among the oldest and most proven forms of alternative energy are the processes for converting coal or natural gas into liquid fuels. A world leader in this field is South African company Sasol (symbol: SSL). Sasol was established in 1950 by the South African government, which wanted to make the country independent of imported oil during the apartheid era. The company has spent decades perfecting its products and now produces a high-quality diesel fuel that is less expensive than ethanol and requires no separate infrastructure. Sasol is currently pursuing plans to establish plants in China, where energy demand is growing quickly.

Ormat Technologies is the fastest-growing geothermal company in the Americas. It is a vertically integrated company that provides power and electricity to the western United States and Hawaii. Geothermal energy, the process of using underground heat to generate electricity, has been the overlooked stepchild of the alternative energy family. Nonetheless, as was discussed in chapter 9, it is a proven energy source that is quite clean and very plentiful, though like all energy sources it will likely run into significant resource constraints.

Ormat is the second-largest builder of geothermal generating plants in the United States, with a significant backlog of projects. It owns more than seventy-five patents and has arguably the best technology in the field. Consequently, the company will be able to grow as fast as it can develop new sources, a rate that we conservatively estimate at 25 percent a year. In addition, Ormat is a leader in recovered energy power generation (REG), the capturing of waste heat generated from industrial processes and converting it into electricity. Demand for REG should also rise along with energy costs. The upside potential in the stock is therefore many times the downside risk.

While FPL is suitable for all investors who want a stake in wind energy, more aggressive investors could consider the more speculative but faster-growing Spanish company Gamesa, and Denmark-based Vesta, the world's two leading turbine manufacturers. At present, both companies have similar valuation metrics, and we expect them to grow by at least 25 percent a year for the next five years or more. We should note that we don't think the increasing price of steel—one of the major constraints on mass development of wind power, as we discussed in chapter 8—will have too great an effect on these companies' growth, because they are both still small and so may be able to avoid such large-scale resource constraints.

Necessary Infrastructure

Of course, simply developing the technology to produce alternative energy will not be enough. Not even building the actual generating stations or fuel production facilities will do it. We also face the monumental task of constructing the infrastructure to make alternative energy available where it is needed.

Infrastructure, it turns out, is already a major stumbling block for the world economy. According to the OECD reports we referred to in chapter 3, the world needs to spend some $2 trillion a year on infrastructure just to maintain adequate freshwater, electricity, telephony, refining capacity, and energy transmission. And that is only for maintenance. It does not even take into account the infrastructure spending required to keep the world economy on even a mildly positive growth trajectory in the years ahead.

We suspect that much of the infrastructure spending envisioned by the OECD will simply not occur. Peak Commodities and Peak Oil will push the costs too high. However, as commodity and oil supplies tighten, infrastructure spending will become a top priority in certain vital areas. In the developing world, for instance, economic growth cannot take place without relentless increases in commodity consumption. Governments in these regions will be forced to sharply increase spending on infrastructure in the effort to raise commodity production. They must build new mines, new oil fields, new water treatment facilities, and new electrical generating plants. In the developed world, including the United States, higher energy prices will similarly lead to new infrastructure spending, at the very least in the areas of oil and alternative energy.

Already the push has begun. For instance, the performance of engineering and construction companies, which do most of the infrastructure building work, is generally tied to oil prices. One reason is that oil companies boost their capital spending when oil prices rise, and then cut back when prices are weak. During the better part of two decades, when oil prices held steady between roughly $15 and $25 a barrel, oil companies pushed the usable life of their infrastructure to the limit. But in 2005, after oil prices had been rising for a year, oil companies began committing to greater capital spending.

The spending surge is taking place on several fronts. First, companies are seeking to upgrade existing infrastructure. They are also building new infrastructure to expand production of established energy sources such as tar sands and liquefied natural gas. Third, they are moving into new forms of energy that were uneconomical when oil prices were lower. The most significant of these are coal-to-gas and coal-to-liquid fuel production (technologies that Sasol is a leader in).

As the commodity squeeze worsens, the engineering and construction industry will be another rewarding area for investors. The potential they offer is really unlimited. Over 50 percent of the profits in this industry derive from oil and gas infrastructure projects, which means any push to increase oil supplies will add to their profits. Within this industry, the company we feel is best positioned to benefit from higher infrastructure spending is Fluor (symbol: FLR).

Within the engineering and construction sector, Fluor is the largest and best-diversified company. Through various subsidiaries, it provides engineering services to a number of industries, including oil and gas, chemicals and petrochemicals, mining and metals, and transportation. As with most E&C companies, the largest part of Fluor's profits comes from its oil and gas projects, where profit margins are highest.

Recently, the number of orders Fluor has been receiving has been growing strongly, with most of them involving oil and gas infrastructure. The company has enjoyed even higher growth from its smaller power division, which serves the electricity generation and transmission industry. Because the U.S. power grid is woefully outdated, growth in this part of the company's operations should remain strong for some time.

Quenching the Inevitable Thirst

Finally, we must reiterate that water and energy are interdependent; you can't have one without the other. So, as one becomes scarcer and more expensive, so does the other. With the world needing to spend close to a half-billion dollars on water infrastructure to meet future needs, we must mention two companies, Veolia and ITT, that specialize in improving supplies of freshwater.

French company Veolia (symbol: VE) is a leader in water infrastructure, ranging from major water treatment facilities to desalination projects. Water prices currently are more heavily subsidized than oil prices. But as water becomes scarcer, deregulation is almost certain, and that will mean higher growth and bigger margins for major players like Veolia. While water infrastructure is the company's major source of revenues, it also has growing stakes in energy, waste disposal, and transportation infrastructure. We should point out that even though water services, especially desalination, are highly energy intensive, the need for water management is indispensable. Companies like Veolia should therefore be able to pass on the increased costs of energy to their customers.

Another company that will benefit from the need for more freshwater is ITT (symbol: ITT), one of the world's largest and most diversified water technology companies. It has a significant market share in water treatment and is a leading manufacturer of equipment for industrial, residential, and commercial water use. In addition, the company is a major provider of defense electronics.

Again, we must caution you that while our recommendations here are based on our current analysis, events may have occurred since these words were written that have created new opportunities or altered our assessment of these companies. We therefore encourage you to get updated information before making investment decisions. As we mentioned before, our newsletter, *The Complete Investor*, is the best source for our latest opinions. Information about it can be found at www.completeinvestor.com.

CHAPTER 18

Our Best Hope:
A Flatter World After All

Benjamin Disraeli once said that change is inevitable. Some changes are insignificant, but others in history have affected the entire planet. Examples include the asteroid that allegedly killed off the dinosaurs, the fall of Rome, and the collapse of communism. And for our generation, we are at the point where a major change is inevitable. The good news is that we have it in our power to control whether the change leads to a better world.

After all, this is not the first time human civilization has been threatened with destruction. History is replete with societies that have come and gone, or come, peaked, and transformed into something different. And despite the seriousness of everything we outlined earlier, we remain steadfastedly optimistic. Thanks to the examples of earlier cultures, we believe we know what humanity must do to avoid total disaster and make the transition to a sustainable civilization. We also believe we know what it will take to remain financially secure during the process.

To review: we pointed out earlier that human civilization begins by harnessing resources, particularly sources of energy. Using the division of labor and hierarchical organization, we have created a complex society that exploits the resources to their fullest potential to bring about many benefits, which we can generally describe as wealth. Naturally, the small percentage of people who occupy the top of various hierarchies, because they control more resources, tend to enjoy more of the wealth.

The problem is that human desire for more wealth or benefits can never be satisfied for long. So over time, the quest for "more" leads to an ever more complex society, which requires ever more resources to sustain it.

Eventually, when all the available resources are fully exploited, production peaks and starts to decline. Resource supplies become too low to support the existing level of complexity, and civilization is forced to change. *This is the situation we find ourselves nearing today.*

There are only two possible ways to combat the problem. One is to increase energy supplies, such as by quickly developing alternative energy sources to replace oil. But, of course, even that will not be enough. No matter how much energy can ultimately be obtained from alternative sources—and we cannot be sure it will ever equal what we currently get from oil—the human desire for more will create more complexity than can be sustained.

In time, the world will have no choice but to become less complex. In some past civilizations, where the upper classes refused to bow to the inevitable until it was too late, this has meant a total collapse, accompanied by great violence and starvation. In other societies, such as certain Mayan communities, affinity and cooperation between classes was stronger. Consequently, they were able to make a difficult but reasonably peaceful transition to a simpler and sustainable social order.

Incidentally, even in a simpler society, individuals can have plenty of opportunities to enjoy a comfortable and even wealthy lifestyle. Our world was a lot simpler back in the 1950s and early 1960s, for example, than it is today. But life was still good for middle-class professionals, and better yet for the wealthiest citizens—even though a typical CEO in 1965 made "only" 40 times the salary of the average employee, rather than 500 times as is often the case nowadays. This dramatic gap has arisen in large part because of the almost innumerable layers between worker and CEO, layers of complexity that contribute next to nothing to the workings of most enterprises or the quality of life in our society.

More important, the necessary decline in complexity, coupled with the immense task of developing alternative energy, will totally change the pathways that lead to financial success in the future. If you have children or grandchildren approaching college age, they will require very different career advice than the previous generation. If you are an investor, you will find you need a whole new strategy to generate profits. In fact, we see signs that the change has already begun.

Occupational Hazards

The year 2008 was not kind to the highest-paid white-collar employees. Thousands and thousands of jobs were cut on Wall Street, some with salaries well into six figures. Many top lawyers did not fare particularly well, either, as the largest profit center for many of the biggest and most prestigious law firms underwent a contraction. The merger and acquisition business was drying up, triggering a decline in the number of hours that many lawyers worked—including hours that were previously valued at $1,000 or more.

Certainly, the layoffs on Wall Street and the decline in billable hours for lawyers came as unwelcome surprises. However, since Wall Street is the hub of our complex society, we are not surprised it is the first place where complexity starts to collapse. In fact, we suspect these reductions are the start of a trend in which traditionally high-paying, desirable professions will find themselves on their way out.

For the past half century, increasing numbers of young people have sought college degrees as tickets to high-paying careers. In 1950, for instance, there were only 2.7 million students enrolled in higher education in the United States—approximately 1.8 percent of the population. By 2002, that number had risen to 16.6 million, or nearly 6 percent of Americans.

Likewise, the number of students in graduate programs has also been increasing. Between 1980 and 2005, the number of master's degrees granted in the United States climbed about two and a half–fold to roughly 575,000. The number of MBAs climbed about five and a half–fold to nearly 143,000, and the number of master's degrees in legal studies rose nearly four and a half–fold. During that same period, the number of doctoral degrees awarded in the U.S. climbed by 62.5 percent, from about 32,000 to over 52,000. The number of PhDs in business nearly doubled, and the number of doctorates in legal professions climbed fivefold.

It is no surprise that legal degrees and MBAs have been among the most sought after for the past generation or so. After all, a typical holder of an MBA (a prerequisite for a top Wall Street position) usually begins his or her business life with an annual salary of at least $80,000. In many cases, that number is well into six figures. The numbers are nearly identical for lawyers. After ten years on the job, the salaries of these professionals will have likely multiplied at least twofold, and five- or sixfold after a generation.

The growth in the number and compensation of educated persons reflects the escalating complexity of our society over the past sixty years. Education is needed to create and manage complexity. The more complex the society, the more educated people occupy the top half of the pyramid, the greater the resources they control, and the higher their compensation. That was as true for priests in ancient Egypt and Sumer as it is for the lawyers, MBAs, and other educated persons who control modern businesses and bureaucracies.

Of course, then as now, educating and compensating a large body of professionals takes a lot of resources. As commodities grow scarcer, those resources will disappear. Or, to put it another way, as inflation rises, profits in the stock market will dwindle, and so will the number of investors. For example, in 1980, only 5.7 percent of U.S. households owned mutual funds. That number rose steadily for the next two decades, peaking along with the bull market in 2001 at 47.8 percent. Since then, it has declined to 43 percent (Sarah Holden, "Trends in Ownership of Mutual Funds in the United States, 2007," *Research Fundamentals*, Investment Company Institute 16.5, November 2007). And as inflation eats into investors' profits, the number of investors will continue to decline. With money flowing out of Wall Street, there will be fewer jobs for professionals, and a lot more downsizing.

Fortunately, not all occupations will suffer the same reductions in numbers and salaries.

The Rise of Skilled Tradesmen

Despite the poor economy in the 2007–2008 period, plenty of jobs were available that did not require a college education. For example, I have a friend who owns a water company that specializes in repairing leaky water systems. Any average high school graduate can master the technology used to make these repairs. Because of the growing water shortages in today's world, the company's growth has far exceeded that of the economy. Indeed, over the past several years the company has been one of the fastest-growing small U.S. franchises.

However, the largest impediment to the company's growth is a shortage of labor. The individuals doing the work have to be skilled. That is, they have to know how to drive trucks and manipulate fairly complex equipment and specialized tools. Again, these are skills that do not require a college degree to learn. Nonetheless, *the shortage of workers in this rapidly growing niche has translated into salaries that in some cases reach into six digits.*

Many other examples today point to the growing importance and compensation for skilled blue-collar labor. A couple of years ago, I attended a dinner celebrating the successful financing of an oil company—one that was destined, incidentally, to become one of the great success stories of the past several years. I was fortunate enough to sit next to several veteran oilmen. They all shared my view that oil supplies were finite and that our ability to increase production is very limited. What they added to my understanding was the fact that oil production is also constrained by another factor—a shortage of skilled labor.

Skilled drill workers have become extremely rare and valued today. My dinner companions said it was not unusual to hire a team of workers to complete a well and, after several days of progress, wake up to find that all of them, without any warning, had packed their bags and left for better-paying jobs. Not surprisingly, the effort to attract and retain workers has pushed salaries to new heights. Skilled oil well workers today can start at $50,000 a year or more and work their way up to six digits in a fairly short time. The same is true for workers in the Canadian tar sands who drive the massive trucks and other equipment. They, too, are in very short supply and the best of them command salaries well over $100,000 annually. Moreover, unlike many lawyers and MBAs, these workers do not have student loans to repay.

We believe the importance of skilled blue-collar workers will only increase as society is forced to invest in the development of alternative energy supplies and the infrastructure to support them. This massive development will be manna for skilled laborers. After all, the necessary infrastructure will not be built by lawyers but by electricians, welders, machinery operators, pipe fitters, technicians, and, especially, engineers. These will be in very short supply and command salaries as high as that of lawyers, MBAs, CFAs, and other traditionally enviable professions.

Consequently, the best trade schools in the country will expand and rise in prestige. They will be the schools parents should encourage their children to enroll in, and the competition will be fierce. Meanwhile, liberal arts schools, and especially schools of law and business, will most likely decline in enrollment.

Perhaps the highest-paid professionals of all will be geologists and applied mathematicians, those who develop the expertise to manipulate materials and discover resource deposits more efficiently. Such skills will be far more important than the ability to draft legal documents or analyze a company's financial statements.

The Nouveaux Riches

As stock market returns dry up over the next ten years, the major stock exchanges will become shadows of their former selves. Trading volume could fall as much as 70 percent simply because investors will stop seeing stocks as a way to make money.

The entire financial industry will scale back. There will be far less need for brokers, fund managers, analysts, and financial advisers. The financial media could downsize as the average person loses interest in the stock market. Rising inflation will also erode the value of bonds and cash investments. Many of today's wealthy will see the value of their assets shrink substantially.

In time, there will be other avenues to wealth than acquiring financial assets. Wealth will be defined not in terms of how many pieces of paper (or blips on a computer) one owns. Instead, it will likely be measured in terms of the volume of commodities one controls. In a sense, we will be turning back the clock to a simpler time.

Consider, for example, two of history's greatest investors, Warren Buffett and John D. Rockefeller. In the second half of the twentieth century, Buffett became one of the two richest living Americans through his extraordinary acumen in the financial markets. His success is a shining example that, in an economy driven by services, managing and mastering complexity brings the greatest rewards.

On the other hand, Rockefeller, America's first billionaire, made his fortune decades earlier, when our world was far less complex. His approach was to accumulate real assets. He built and bought up oil refineries, thus gaining control of what would become the world's major energy source. As Peak Commodities unfolds and resources grow scarce, the ability to find and accumulate resources will once again become the most important route to riches.

Incidentally, if we are right in thinking that things will become much less complex in the future, then we can expect the process of investing will become simpler as well. For instance, in Rockefeller's time, buying an asset required little more than a few pieces of paper and one or two lawyers. In today's world, any significant purchase takes a whole team of investment bankers, accompanied by additional teams of lawyers and accountants. If we survive the coming transition, all this complexity will likely disappear. The next generation of self-made multimillionaires and billionaires will be people who develop the skill of spotting valuable resources, often in their own backyard, and acquiring control of them without the help of flocks of Wall Street professionals, all of whom in the past would have demanded their cut.

Ironically, while sky-high inflation will cripple financial returns and destroy much wealth, it will also wipe out debt, which could be a boon to those who are now strapped. A simpler society will mean all the leverage and derivative products—the SPEs, SIVs, CDOs that have resulted in several major financial crises in the past decade and continue to hang over us like the sword of

Damocles—will vanish from the scene. And while the investment choices will be few, those few will promise great riches.

Flat World

We mentioned earlier Thomas Friedman's thesis that the world is becoming flatter, that the advantages the United States and the developed world have had in the past are disappearing as the entire world develops. Our contention with Friedman is that the world simply does not have enough resources for 7 billion people to enjoy a lifestyle equal to that of today's American middle class.

Nonetheless, the world could and perhaps should flatten; income disparities between nations and classes will need to equalize, or at least lessen. However, the process will likely mean that lifestyles in the developed world will decline as those in developing nations rise.

As the United States conducts the necessary research to see how our energy and resource needs can be better fulfilled, it will be in our interest to transfer this knowledge to the developing world. If we can help developing nations find and use resources more efficiently while simultaneously helping ourselves, it will buy not just us but the entire world more time to develop alternative energies and reach sustainability.

Of course, developing nations will continue to increase their resource consumption. As we have pointed out, they have no choice. This will mean that the developed world will have to adopt even stricter conservation strategies to minimize shortfalls. We sincerely hope an international cooperative effort can be made to ease the transition to a flatter world. Otherwise, it is too easy to imagine resource wars breaking out, resulting in catastrophic losses and the utter collapse of civilization.

In time, our complex, information-based economy will revert to a more industrial one. As the financial assets of the wealthy are destroyed by inflation, and as the salaries of non-college-educated workers rise, the social order will devolve into a simpler form in which income differences are dramatically reduced.

One of the casualties of the transition will be the idea that more is better. Modern economic theory, based on the supremacy of capitalism and the notion that an individual's worth is defined by how much he or she can afford to consume, will have little place in the new world. Such ideas just will not work in a world where resource constraints are tangible and severe. As Stephen Marglin put it in *The Dismal Science: How Thinking Like an Economist Undermines Community* (Harvard University Press, 2008), in summarizing the work of environmental economists:

> Mainstream economics is all well and good when the impact of the economy on the environment and the resource base is small, but the same economics becomes irrelevant when we are up against ecological constraints.... Economic growth transforms the economy to the point that mainstream economics is no longer adequate to diagnose problems or prescribe solutions.... With growth, externalities that might be marginal annoyances can become threats to survival.

Our point is not simply that Peak Commodities will require economists to change their obsolete ways of thinking. Rather, it is that capitalism may no longer work if the world is forced to start rationing and allocating resources. Unrestrained capitalism would bring about the Tragedy of the Commons scenario, in which individual agents, pursuing their own self-interest, destroy the resource base and bring about a total economic collapse.

Instead, we may come to define wealth in terms other than consumption. Certainly, material wealth is necessary for meeting our needs for food, clothing, shelter, and medicine. We hope that in time the world's population escapes from poverty and fulfills these needs. However, as A. H. Maslow pointed out in 1946, once human beings achieve the necessities of life, they can easily move on to the pursuit of other goals, such as community building (what we now call social capital), personal needs such as self-esteem and confidence, and, finally, self-actualization, in which they become fully integrated persons. We may in time see a world in which human happiness is defined not just by wealth but by the contribution one makes to one's community, the skills one attains, creative achievements, and the acquisition of wisdom.

At any rate, it is clear that if civilization is to survive the resource crunch and prevent Game Over, government will need to play a bigger role in the economy, to make sure resources are directed toward projects that will promote civilization's long-term sustainability. Our challenge will be more sociological than economic, in that we will have to work hard to preserve individual freedoms in a world desperate to survive and transitioning to a new order.

In the end, life may not be too bad for future generations. Civilization, on a best-case basis, will adopt a much simpler structure in which inequalities are dramatically lessened. A vastly diminished Wall Street and its accompaniments will be one feature of a less complex society.

A simpler society can mean a more productive one. And if the United States can regain its energy independence, the rest of its competitive advantages could be reobtained in the process. In other words, if we do everything right, we will face a minimum of a decade or more of utter turbulence that will stress our society far more than either a major war or depression, but the pain may be worth it. For at the end of this inflation flood could be a rainbow of plentiful energy, food, and a simpler life for the entire world. We can't promise, but if we can get through the next decade or more, the days that follow could resemble the prosperity of the 1950s.

Index

Absolute Peak Commodities, 7, 29, 33, 163
  buying time until, 8, 113–23
  timing of, 79
Absolute Peak Energy, 29
Absolute Peak Oil, 7, 22–23, 32, 33, 163
  buying time until, 8, 113–23
  changes to expect prior to reaching, 23
  timing of, 22–23, 79
acid rain, 41
Africa, 209
  investment opportunities in, 194
Agnico-Eagle (symbol: AEM), 185
agrarian societies, 61
AIG, ix
airline stocks, investment in, 202–203
Alaskan oil fields, 150
"Alberta's Tar Sands Are Soaking Up Too
  Much Water," 38
Alcoa, 29–30, 88
alternative energies, ix, 5, 7–8, 86–112, 131,
    148, 223
  buying time, see buying time
  complexity, and the shortfall in resources,
    68–76
  cost of transition to, 81–82
  false assumption about, 2
  focus of energy research, 80–81
  infrastructure for, building of, 81, 88
  investing in, and its infrastructure,
    213–20
  key questions in evaluating, 87
  Manhattan Project-like effort to develop,
    5, 80–82

resource shortages as factor when
    evaluating, 5–6, 87, 88
  roadblocks to action, 82–85
  trade-offs, examining, 6, 87
  transition to, 79–80, 81–82
  water dependence of, 37, 40–41, 42, 90,
    91, 92, 94–95, 104
  window of opportunity for developing, 23
  see also specific forms of alternative energy
aluminum, 29–30, 103
American Century zero coupon bond
    funds, 204
American Depository Receipts (ADRs), 200
American Silver (symbol: PAAS), 187–88
AMEX Gold Miners Index, 184
Anglo Platinum (symbol: AGPPY), 188, 194
Anthony, Scott D., 72–73
antimony, world reserves of, 25, 26
Arctic National Wildlife Refuge (ANWR), 15
Atlanta, Georgia, 41
Australia, 95, 193
  BRAC nations, investing in, 190–94
  strength of currency of, 148, 178, 191
automobile companies, investment in,
    202–203
automobiles, 108–12
  gasoline, see gasoline
  hybrids, 109, 110
  natural-gas powered, 5, 86, 87, 109, 111–12
  obstacles of converting from gasoline-run,
    109–12
  wind energy to fuel, 96, 97, 108–109
Automotive Digest, 109

bailout of the financial industry, 2008, ix
Baker Hughes (symbol: BHI), 198
Baku-Tbilisi-Ceyhan (BTC) pipeline, 206
balance of trade, 142
banking system, 154
    derivatives, and subprime mortgage
        crisis, 155
bankruptcies, consumer, 152, 154
Barrick Gold (symbol: ABX), 184–85
Bartis, James T., 38
Bear Stearns, ix, 154, 155
Beaty, Ross, 187
Berkshire Hathaway (symbol: BRK/B), 203
Bernanke, Ben, 156
BHP Billiton (symbol: BHP), 194, 195
biofuels and biomass, 105–108, 215–16
bitumen, 91
"Blood Barrels: Why Oil Wealth Fuels
    Conflict," 145
Bloomberg, Michael, 86
blue-collar workers, skilled, 226–28
BMO (Canadian investment firm), 65
bonds, 228
    government, 172
    long-term, 170
    returns on, 172–73, 177, 181
    standard advice of financial planners,
        175
    zero coupon, 196, 204
BRAC (Brazil, Russia, Australia, Canada)
        nations, investing in, 190–94
    balancing risk and reward, 193
    exchange-traded funds (ETFs), 192, 193
Brazil, 1, 190, 192–93
    strength of currency of, 148
BRIC (Brazil, Russia, India, China)
        nations, 190
Brown, Lester R., 36, 37
budget deficits, 143, 144
budget surplus of 1950s, 142, 143
Buffett, Warren, 79, 203, 228–29
Bushveld Igneous Complex, South Africa,
        188
BusinessWeek, 72–73
buying time, 8, 113–23
    with advance applied mathematics, 8, 114,
        120–23
    with energy conservation, 8, 114, 115–17
    with geological exploration, 119–20, 123
    by reducing complexity, 8, 114
    technological innovation and, 117–19

Cameco (symbol: CCJ), 200
Canada, 193
    BRAC nations, investing in, 190–94
    strength of Canadian dollar, 148,
        178, 191
    tax code, 199
Canadian Oil Sands Trust (COSWF), 199
Canadian tar sands, 19, 37–38, 199, 227
capitalism, 1, 231
    longevity of Western-style, 179
Carioca oil field, 16, 33
Carter, Jimmy, 150
CEO compensation, 224
Chad, 145
change, resistance to, 83, 124, 125–26
chemical companies, 202–203
China, 142
    as BRIC nation, 190
    consumption and growing middle class
        in, 45–52
    defense expenditures, 209
    economic growth of, 43, 45, 46–52, 159
    freshwater tables in, 36
    gold as savings vehicle in, 179
    international resource exploration, 208
    nuclear power in, 94
    vehicles per person, 1, 45
    wages in, 169–70, 190
    water contamination in, 38
    yuan, 169–70, 190
Christensen, Clayton M., 72–73
chromium, world reserves of, 25, 26
civilization, collapse of our, see Game Over
        (collapse of our civilization)
civil wars in resource-rich undeveloped
        nations, 145
climate change, see global warming
Club of Rome, 126–28
coal, 64, 90, 92–94, 97, 214
    conversion to liquid fuels, 216–17
    environmental costs of, 17, 41, 93
    gasification, 87, 90, 93–94, 219
    prices, 92, 93
Cohen, Joel, 37
Coifman, Ronald, 120–21, 123
Cold War, 207
Collapse (Diamond), 130
collapse of civilization, see Game Over
        (collapse of our civilization)
Collapse of Complex Societies, The (Tainter),
        62–63

collateralized debt obligations (CDOs), 155, 229

Collier, Paul, 145

Colorado River, 36

combination of resource shortages, 5–6, 10
  evaluation of alternative energies and, 5–6, 87, 88
  vicious circles and, ix, 6, 27–33, 40, 59, 79, 95, 99, 100, 103

Coming Economic Collapse, The (Leeb et al.), 130, 160, 161

commodities, x
  advantages of undeveloped nations resource-rich nations, 140
  the combination of resource shortages, 5–6, 10
  defense spending to maintain access to, 144–46
  investing in, *see* investing
  rationing of, 8, 231
  as road to wealth, 228–29
  shortages of, 3, 5, 9
  U.S. imports of, 140
  vicious circles, *see* vicious circles, combination of resource shortages and
  see also individual commodities

commodity prices, x, 172
  basket of currencies as basis for, 148
  inflation and, 137–38, 162
  rising, 3, 128–29, 169
  weakening of the dollar and, 147–48

communism, fall of, 178, 179

complacency, 115, 124

Complete Investor, The (investment newsletter), 196, 221

complexity of societies, 58–67, 221
  buying time by reducing, 8, 114
  downside of, 62–64
  higher education and, 225
  historical perspective, 60–62
  leading to collapse, 63–64
  oil production and, 64–67, 114
  scaling back of, to simpler societies, 9, 60, 223–24, 229–31, 232
  Wall Street, and the shortfall in resources, 68–76

Congressional Joint Economic Committee, 115

conservation of energy, 8, 114, 115–17, 131, 150

construction costs, rising, 31

Consumer Price Index (CPI), 137, 139, 156, 170

copper, 103, 195
  world reserves of, 25, 26

corn, ethanol from, 105–106, 107

"Costs Surge for Building Power Plants," 31

Cummings, William J., 16

currencies
  Chinese yuan, 169–70, 190
  history of, as financial assets, 179
  pricing of commodities in basket of currencies, 148, 178
  of resource-rich nations, 148, 178, 189–90
  the U.S. dollar, *see* dollar, U.S.
  see also BRAC (Brazil, Russia, Australia, Canada) nations, investing in; BRIC (Brazil, Russia, India, China) nations

data, technological advances in processing, 117–19

Davies, Paul, 83

debt levels, U.S., 161, 177, 229
  Federal Reserve's ability to control inflation and, 152, 155–58, 160
  as percentage of GDP, 151–52

defense spending, 144–46
  investing in defense sector, 205–12
  leading companies in defense industry, 211–12
  as percentage of GDP, 210

defensive investments
  to avoid, 200–203
  worth owning, 203–204

deflation, x, 143, 160, 187
  gold as investment during periods of, 9, 181, 187, 189, 196
  investing and, 176–77
  oil and energy stocks and, 196
  zero coupon bonds as hedge against, 204

Defying the Market (Leeb et al.), 117, 167

denial, 82–83, 124, 128–30, 131–33

depressions, 163
  Great Depression, 143, 155–56, 163, 181, 186, 187

derivatives, 154–55, 229–30

developing countries, 44–57
  energy consumption of, 52–54, 116–17
  flatter world, transition to, 230
  globalization and, 56–57
  gold as savings vehicle in, 179

developing countries (*cont.*)
  growing middle class and consumption in,
    1, 36–37, 45–52
  impact of world recession on, 159
  industrialization of, 36
  outsourcing to, 138
  rapid growth in, 8, 43–44, 45–52, 107,
    158, 159
  reliance on, for important resources, 4
  resource shortages halting growth of, 8, 44
  use of their own resources, implications
    of, 54–56
  wage-commodity vicious circle, 139
  water demands of, 36
  see also individual countries
Diamond, Jared, 130
disaster, upside of, 133–34
*Dismal Science: How Thinking Like an
  Economist Undermines Community, The*
  (Marglin), 231
diversified portfolio, 175–76
division of labor, 61, 62, 222–23
dollar, U.S.
  Canadian dollar's near parity with, 191
  as reserve currency, 148, 178
  strength of, 117, 142
  weakening, 147–48, 172, 178, 191, 192
"Draining Our Future: The Growing
  Shortage of Freshwater," 36, 37
drought, 35–36, 95, 106
Duke Energy, 31
Durkheim, Emile, 125

East Timor, 145
economic growth
  in Africa, 194
  in the developing world, *see* developing
    countries, rapid growth in
  false assumption about, 2, 140
  implications of Western-style, in
    developing countries, 56, 140–41
  predictions of future world, 2–3
education, occupational shifts and, 225,
  226, 228
energy conservation, 8, 114, 115–17, 131, 150
energy prices
  coal, 92, 93
  oil, *see* oil prices
  vicious circles, *see* vicious circles,
    combination of resource
    shortages and

energy research
  focused on the big pictures, 80–81
  U.S. government expenditures on, 79
Energy Resources (symbol: EGRAF), 200, 215
Eni (oil company), 21
entitlement programs, 144, 146–47
  false assumption about funding, 2
environmental regulations, 67
ethanol, 105–108, 216
exchange-traded funds (ETFs), 183, 184,
  192, 193
Exelon (symbol: EXC), 215, 216
ExxonMobil, 16, 31–32, 66

false assumptions underlying U.S. economic
  system, 2
Fannie Mae, ix, 157
Federal Reserve, 134, 150–54, 155–58, 159,
  162, 176
  fed funds rate, chart of, 153
  recession of 2001 and, 152–53
  under Volcker, 150–51, 154
fertilizer prices, 106
Fidelity Select Gold Fun (FSAGX), 184
financial industry, *see* Wall Street
financial strength of the U.S., waning,
  141–44, 158–59
First Solar, 102, 215
fiscal policy, U.S., 143
flooding, 36
Fluor (symbol: FLR), 219–20
food supply, 37, 61
  conflict between biofuels and, 105–106,
    107, 216
Foreign Affairs, 21, 107, 145
fossil fuels, *see specific fossils fuels, e.g.* coal; oil
FPL Group (symbol: FPL), 215, 216
France, nuclear power in, 41
Freddie Mac, ix, 157
Friedman, Thomas L., 5, 56–57, 87–89, 230

Galison, Peter, 83
Game Over (collapse of our civilization), 3,
  9, 10, 13, 23, 44, 79, 163, 223
Gamesa (symbol: GCTAF), 215, 217–18
Ganges River, 36
gasoline
  ethanol and, 105–108
  obstacles of converting from gasoline-run
    cars, 109–12
  prices, 4

taxes, 116
tax holiday, 5, 116
Gates, Bill, 79, 187
Gazprom (symbol: OGZPY), 199–200, 206
General Dynamics, 211, 212
General Motors Volt, 110–11
geological exploration, buying time with,
    119–20, 123
geologists, 228
Georgia, Russian invasion of, 205–206, 209
geothermal energy, 104–105, 217
German mark, 179
Ghawar oil field, 20, 22
globalization and the developing world,
    56–57
global warming, 93, 130–33
gold, investing in, 9, 178–86, 187, 189, 196
    bull market in, 182–83
    coins or bullion, 183
    exchange-traded funds (ETFs), 183, 184
    gold stocks, 183–85
    history of, 179–80
    long-term price chart, 180–81
    mutual funds, 184
    -oil ratio, 182
    periods of greatest returns, 181
    as reserve asset, 179
Goldman Sachs, 129–30, 155
Goodstein, David, 17
Gore, Al, 130
Gott, J. Richard, III, 178–79
Government Accountability Office
    (GAO), 146
government spending, 144–47, 148,
    161, 213
Great Depression, 143, 155–56, 163
    gold as investment during, 181
    silver as investment in, 186, 187

Halliburton (symbol: HAL), 198
Harbin, China, 38
Hardin, Garrett, 132–33
Hawking, Stephen, 83–84
health issues, fossil fuels and, 92–93,
    94, 97
Herbert, Bob, 115
hierarchical organization, 61–62, 222–23, 224
Hoeffler, Anke, 145
Hoffman, Dr. Allan R., 40
Holden, Sarah, 226
Honda, natural-gas powered Civic, 111–12

Hot, Flat and Crowded: Why We Need a Green
    Revolution — and How It Can Renew
    America (Friedman), 87–89
housing crisis, subprime mortgages and, 119,
    154–55, 160–61
housing prices, 153–54, 157, 160–61
"How Biofuels Could Starve the Poor," 107
How Many People Can the Earth Support?
    (Cohen), 37
Hubbert, M. King, 14
Hughes, David, 92
Hunt brothers, 186
Hussein, Saddam, 209
Hydrocarbon Depletion Study Group, 17
hydrogen, 91, 108, 109

Iceland, geothermal energy in, 104
Ichalkaranji, India, 38
Image and Logic (Galison), 83
Impala Platinum (symbol: IMPUY),
    188, 194
Inconvenient Truth, An, 130
India
    as BRIC nation, 190
    consumption and growing middle class
        in, 45–52
    currency of, 190
    economic growth of, 43, 45, 46–52
    freshwater tables in, 36
    gold as savings vehicle in, 179
    vehicles per person, 1, 45
    wages in, 169, 190
    water pollution in, 38
indium, world reserves of, 25, 26
Indus River, 36
industrial revolution, 64
inflation, x, 83, 134, 137–63, 168, 228
    depletion of reserves of critical minerals
        and metals and, 26
    derivatives and, 154–55
    economic growth in the developing world
        and, 140–41
    false assumption about ability to
        control, 2
    Federal Reserve policy and, 134, 143,
        150–54, 155–58, 159, 176
    government spending and, 144–47
    investment strategies and, see investing
        in 1950s, 142
    past solutions, viability of, 149–63
    predictions of future, 2–3, 8, 13, 24, 54, 148

inflation (*cont.*)
  real returns on investments and, 173,
    177–78
  reasons for relatively tame, 169–70
  scenarios, 159–62
  transition to alternative energies and,
    82
  wage-commodity vicious circle, 139
  waning economic power of the U.S. and,
    141–44
infrastructure, 2
  for alternative energies, 81, 218–20
  water, 40, 220–21
"Institutional Evolution in the Holocene:
  The Rise of Complex Societies," 61
International Atomic Energy Agency,
  200
investing, 9, 229
  in alternative energies and its
    infrastructure, 213–20
  in BRAC nations, 190–94
  comparison of 1970s, 1990s, and 2000s,
    167–71
  in defense sector, 205–12
  defensive plays to avoid, 200–203
  deflation and, 176–77
  diversified portfolio, 175–76
  financial advisors, shortcomings of
    traditional advice of, 171–77
  in oil stocks, 196–200
  in precious metals, 178–88
  real returns, 173, 177–78
  in water infrastructure companies,
    220–21
  world's best resource stocks, 194–96
  see also individual investments, e.g. bonds;
    gold, investing in
Iran, 140–41, 149–50, 167, 210
  economic growth rate of, 1, 141
  energy consumption of, 1, 141
  Iranian Revolution, 149
  -Iraq War, 149
  nuclear program, 140–41
"Iranian Petroleum Crisis and United States
  National Security, The," 141
Iraq, 210
  -Iran War, 149
  oil production, 151
Iraq war, 79
  access to Iraqi oil and, 145, 209
iron ore, 5, 6–7, 25, 89, 98, 99

iShares Silver Trust (symbol: SLV),
  187
ITT (symbol: ITT), 220–21

Jack 2 field, Gulf of Mexico, 16
Jacobson, Mark, 96–98, 101, 108–109
Japan, 142
"Justice Seeking and Loot Seeking in Civil
  War," 145

kerogen, 91, 92
Kinross Gold (symbol: KGC), 185–86
Kleinfeld, Klaus, 88
Kyoto Protocol, 130

Lake Tai, 38
large cap stocks, 167–70
lawyers, 224, 225
lead, world reserves of, 25, 26
learning curve effect, 98–99, 104
Lehman Brothers, ix, 155
Limits of Growth, The (Club of Rome),
  126–28
lithium-based batteries, 110
Lockheed Martin, 211, 212
Long-Term Capital Management, 119
L-Communications, 211, 212
lung diseases, 92

macro- and microeconomics, division in
  focus of, 84–85
managerial fix interpretation, 132
Mann, Paul, 18
Marglin, Stephen, 231
market economy, 61
  transition to alternative energies and, 80
Market Vectors Gold Miners ETF (symbol:
  GDX), 184
Maslow, A. H., 232
mathematics, advance applied, 8, 114,
  120–23, 228
Mayan civilization, 63
MBAs, 225
meat consumption, 37
Medicare, 146
metals
  complacency about diminishing shortfalls
    in, 27
  vicious circles, *see* vicious circles,
    combination of resource shortages and
  world reserves of industrial, 25–26

Middle East, 209
    reaching Peak Oil and, 19–22
    Western-style economies in, implications
        of development of, 56, 140–41
    see also individual nations
military budget, *see* defense spending
minerals
    complacency about diminishing shortfalls
        in, 27
    geological exploration, 119–20
    investing in, 178–88
    vicious circles, *see* vicious circles,
        combination of resource shortages and
    world reserves of industrial, 25–26
mining
    environmental damage from, 92, 93, 94
    freshwater needed in, 6
MIT, 105
Modern Portfolio Theory, 175
monetary policy, 134, 143, 150–54, 155–58,
    159, 162, 177
money supply (M3), 157
Morgan Stanley, 155
mortgage-backed securities (MBSs), 155
mortgages, home, 153–54
    subprime, 119, 154–55, 160–61
Mugabe, Robert, 209
multistage flash distillation, 39
Mutual Assured Destruction (MAD), 207
Myanmar, 145

Al-Naimi, Sheikh, 19, 31
national debt, U.S., 142, 143–44
    false assumption about, 2
National Oilwell Varco (symbol: NOV), 198
NATO, 205, 206
natural gas, 106
    automobiles powered by, 5, 86, 87, 109,
        111–12
    exploration, 66
    hydrogen from, 91
Nature, 40–41, 83, 131, 178–79
net energy gain of an alternative energy, 87
    solar energy, 101, 102
New Scientist, 17
New York Times, 31, 86, 115
    Week in Review, 167
nickel
    world reserves of, 25, 26
Nixon, Richard M., 168
Northrop Grumman (symbol: NOC), 211

North Sea oil production, 18, 150
NovaGold's Galore Creek project,
    Canada, 30
nuclear power, 94–96, 200, 214, 216
    Iran and, 140–41
    safety issues, 96
    water requirements of reactors, 37, 40–41,
        94–95

occupations
    in jeopardy, 224–26
    skilled tradesmen, rise of, 226–28
offshore drilling, 15
oil, 13–24, 64
    Absolute Peak Oil, *see* Absolute Peak Oil
    the combination of resource shortages,
        5–6, 10
    crisis of 1970, 128, 149
    estimates of earth's original resources, 15–16
    exploration, 16, 17–18, 32, 114, 120
    false assumption about world reserves, 2
    gold-oil ratio, 182
    heavy, high-sulfur oil, 16
    Iraq war and, 145
    light, sweet oil, 16
    mismatch between world supply and
        demand, 18
    Peak Oil, *see* Peak Oil
    rationing of, 8
    scientists' views on oil reserves, 17–18
    from tar sands, *see* tar sands, oil from
    U.S. imports of, 55, 140
oil companies
    investment in, 32
    oil service companies, 129, 197–99, 202
    profits, 31–32
    short-term traders in shares of, 75
    tax breaks for, 66–67
    valuation of, 129
    Wall Street, complexity, and, 68–73
    windfall profits tax on, 5
Oil Factor, The (Leeb et al.), 130
oil prices, 22, 93, 172
    free markets and, 5
    futures market, 73–74
    increases in, 14, 219
    inflation and, 137–38
    investments to avoid during rising,
        202–203
    in 1950s, 142
    in past energy crises, 149–50

oil prices (*cont.*)
  speculators and traders, 5, 73–76, 129
  spot market, 73
  in 2008, 4, 129, 138
  Wall Street forecasts for, 129–30
oil production, 32, 151, 197
  complexity and, 64–67, 114
  costs of increasing, 31
  drilling proponents, 4
  energy needs of developing world and, 53
  in past energy crises, 149–50
  Peak Oil, *see* Peak Oil
  skilled labor and, 227
  technology and, 14–15
  U.S., 15, 18, 21, 64–65, 140, 142
oil refineries, regulatory environment and
  construction of, 67
oil shale, 90, 91, 94
"Oil Shale Development in the United
  States: Prospects and Policy Issues,"
  38
oil stocks, 196–200
OPEC (Organization of Petroleum
  Exporting Countries)
  dollar as reserve currency for, 148
  oil embargo of 1973, 149
  oil reserves of, 20
optimism, American, 144
Organisation for Economic Co-Operation
  and Development (OECD), 40, 218
Ormat Technologies (symbol: ORA),
  215, 217
Out of Gas: The End of the Age of Oil
  (Goodstein), 17
outsourcing of production and services, wage
  costs and, 138, 169

Pachganga River, 38
Parkinson, Cyril, 62
Peak Coal, 92
Peak Oil, 14, 15, 22, 32
  arguments of critics of, 14–15
  defining, 14
  estimates of when it will be reached, 18–22
P/E ratios, 201–202
Petaquilla's copper project, Panama, 30
PetroChina, 208
phosphorus, 106
photovoltaics, thin film, 101, 102–103
Pickens, T. Boone, 5, 86, 109, 111

platinum and platinum group metals
  (PGMs), 109
  investing in, 185, 186, 187, 188, 194
  world reserves of, 25, 26
Plato, 61
postindustrial countries, 51
potash, 106–107
*Prize: The Epic Quest for Oil, Money & Power,
  The* (Yergin), 64–65
*Proceedings of the National Academy of
  Science,* 141
Producer Price Index (PPI), 137, 170
professions, future of high-paying, 224–26
"Put Investors in Their Place," 73

rationing of commodities, 8, 231
Raytheon (symbol: RTN), 211–12
recessions, 8, 13, 24, 83
  Federal Reserve policy and, 134, 150–54,
    155–58, 159, 162
  high debt levels and, 152, 153, 155–56
  of 2001, 152–53
  Volcker's monetary policy and, 150–51
recovered energy power generation
  (RDG), 217
regulatory environment, 8
  costs of compliance, 67
  of U.S. oil industry, 64–65
Reicher, Dan, 115
reinsurance industry, 203
Renaissance, 64
renewable energies, *see* alternative energies;
  *specific renewable energies, e.g. solar
  energy; wind energy*
resource shortages, 13–76
  combination of, *see* combination of
    resource shortages
  The Limits of Growth warns of, 126–28
  see also individual resources
reverse osmosis distillation, 39, 40
Rhine River, contamination of, 35, 38
Richerson, Peter J., 61
Rio Tinto (symbol: RTP), 194–95
Rockefeller, John D., 229
Roman Empire, collapse of, 63–64
Ross, Michael L., 145
Runge, C. Ford, 107
Russia, 192–93, 205–208
  BRAC nations, investing in, 190–94
  defense expenditures, 209
  invasion of Georgia, 205–206, 209

oil production, 129
risk of investments in, 185–86, 200

Sandford Bernstein, 22
sanitation, 37
Sasol (symbol: SSL), 215, 216–17, 219
Saudi Arabia, 209–10
Saudi Arabian oil, 19–22, 31, 129
   threats to, 133
"Saving Our Future Requires Tough Choices
   Today," 146
Schlumberger (symbol: RIG), 198–99
Science, 97
Securities and Exchange Commission
   (SEC), 69
self-actualization, 232
Senauer, Benjamin, 107
September 11, 2001, terrorist attacks of, 152
silicon, 101, 102
silver, 119–20, 162
   investing in, 186, 187
   world reserves of, 25, 26
Simmons, Matthew, 20, 112
Simons, James, 76
Simpson, Jeffrey, 38
skilled tradesmen, rise of, 226–28
small cap stocks, 167
social capital, 232
Social Security, 142–43, 146
solar energy, 89, 100–104, 214
   geographic differences in effectiveness of,
      102
   solar cells, 6, 100–101, 102–103
   solar collectors, 100, 103–104
   storage of, 101–102
Songhua River, 38
South America, access to resources of, 209
Southern Copper (symbol: PCU), 195
soybeans, 105
SPDR Gold Shares (symbol: GLD), 183
speculators, 5, 73–76, 129
steel, 6, 87, 88–89, 98, 99, 211, 217–18
Stern, Roger, 141
stock market
   decline in number of investors in, 226
   future of, 228
   technology bubble, 143, 152, 161
stocks
   defensive investments worth owning, 203
   defensive plays to avoid, 200–203
   gold, 183–85

large cap, 167–70
oil, 196–200
past returns on, 172
silver mining, 187–88
small cap, 167
world's best resource, 194–96
see also exchange-traded funds (ETFs)
stress, change-induced, 125–26
STRIPS (Separate Trading of Registered
   Interest and Principal of Securities), 204
subprime mortgages, 119, 154–55, 160–61
sub-Saharan Africa, economic growth in,
   194
Suicide (Durkheim), 125
sustainable economy, 13, 44, 127

Tainter, Joseph, 62–63
tantalum, world reserves of, 25, 26
tar sands, oil from, 16, 90–93, 227
   Canadian, 19, 37–38, 199
   water inputs, 38, 90
taxes, 65–66
   on carbon-based energy, 116–17
   energy exploration and uncertainty about,
      66
   gasoline, 5, 116
   government spending and, 146–47
technology
   buying time and, 117–19
   false assumption about long-term problem
      solving with, 2, 65
   Peak Oil and, 14–15
   stock prices and the technology bubble,
      143, 152, 161
Technology Review, 110–11
"Tectonic Setting of 79 Giant Oil and Gas
   Fields Discovered from 2000-2007:
   Implications for Future Discovery
   Trends," 18
tellurium, 5–6, 102–103
terrorism
   nuclear power and, 96
   September 11, 2001, 152
Texas Railroad Commission, 64
Three Mile Island nuclear power plant, 94
tin, world reserves of, 25, 26
titanium, 41–42
Tocqueville Gold Fund (TGLDX), 184
Too Little Oil for Global Warming (Hydrogen
   Depletion Study Group), 17
Toyota Prius, 110

trade deficit, false assumption about reversing the, 2
Tragedy of the Commons, 132–33, 231
transistors, 98
transportation systems, oil-run, 14
"Trends in Ownership of Mutual Funds in the United States, 2007," 226
tulip bulbs as financial assets, 179
tunnel vision, 83–85, 98
Twilight in the Desert (Simmons), 20

unemployment, 150–51, 161
U.S. Department of Energy, 19, 169
United States Geological Survey, 41
Uppsala University, 17
uranium, 200
    nuclear power and, 95–96, 200
    world reserves of, 25, 26

Vadodara, India, 38
Veolia (symbol VE), 220
Vesta (symbol: VWSYF), 215, 217–18
vicious circles, 163
    combination of resource shortages and, ix, 6, 27–33, 40, 42, 59, 79, 95, 99, 100, 103
    fable illustrating, 27–29
    two-way street between metal and mineral prices and energy prices, 30–33
    wage-commodity, 139
    warning signs, 29–30
Vishwamitri River, 38
Volcker, Paul, 150–51, 154

wages
    -commodity vicious circle, 139
    in developing world, 138, 139, 169–70
    inflation and, 139
Wald, Matthew L., 31
Walker, David M., 146–47
Wall Street
    bailout of 2008, ix
    complexity, and the shortfall in resources, 68–76
    computerized trading, 118–19
    forecasts for oil prices, 129–30
    future of, 228
    job losses, 224

short-term perspective of, 69, 72–73
valuation of oil stocks, 129
Wall Street Journal, 88–89
water as resource, 6, 34–42
    agriculture and, 36–37
    alternative energies dependent on, 37, 40–41, 42, 90, 91, 92, 94–95, 104
    conservation efforts, 39–40
    contamination of, 35, 36, 38–39, 42
    drought, 35–36, 40, 41
    flooding, 36
    freshwater supply, 35
    industrial demand for, 36, 37, 38
    infrastructure, 40, 220–21
    investing in infrastructure companies, 220–21
    purification technologies, 39, 40, 95, 220
    safe drinking water, 37, 38
    shifts in location of freshwater, 36
    water cycle, 35
Watson, Thomas, 118
wealth
    new avenues to, 228–29
    redefining, 231–32
wildcatting, 21
wind energy, 5, 6–7, 86, 89, 96–99, 108–109, 214, 216
    steel (iron ore) requirements for wind turbines, 6–7, 87, 98, 99
    storage of, 101
windfall profits tax on oil companies, 5
window of opportunity for solving resource shortage problems, 3–4, 23
    buying time, *see* buying time
"Winning Hand, The," 115
wood as energy source, 214
World Bank, 52, 145
World Is Flat, The (Friedman), 56–57

XTO Energy (symbol: XTO), 200

Yellow River, 36
Yergin, Daniel, 64–65
Yom Kippur War, 149
Yucca Mountain, 96

zero coupon bonds, 196, 204
zinc, world reserves of, 25, 26

Acknowledgments

The research and ideas for this book are my own. But to translate my thinking into sufficiently readable form, I relied on four people whose contributions were so important that I felt all deserved credit as coauthors. Donna Leeb and Glen Strathy were essential in taking my research and organizing it into a coherent narrative that pulled all my ideas together, ensuring that my arguments were developed and highlighted in a clear, accessible way. My son Will Leeb contributed chapter 3, on water, and filled in the blanks in describing the mathematical basis for the work of Ronald Coifman. Genia Turanova reviewed all the material and provided all the charts and graphs. I felt that simply thanking these four would have been totally insufficient recognition of their critical roles.

I do want to thank several others, including the entire staff at Leeb Group. In particular, I am grateful to my assistant, Sarah Stone, for her help in coordinating the project and to my associate Patrick DeSouza, who contributed to my understanding of how economic security and national security are intertwined. For his many thought-provoking comments, I am grateful to my friend Tom Kaplan, who has a preternatural gift for spotting long-term trends and is one of the most successful commodity investors around. And I also benefited, as always, from the many spirited discussions I have had with three exceptionally bright people: Steve Rittenberg, Noah Shaw, and Herb Wyman.

Finally, once again I want to thank my longtime agent and friend Al Zuckerman, who now deserves credit for encouraging and making possible the past six books I have written. And I am very grateful to our editor, Rick Wolff, whose comments were always pertinent and helpful and who kept us acutely aware of the need to get the book done on time. And I also want to thank the extraordinary staff at Business Plus, especially Mari Okuda, Bob Castillo, Tracy Martin, and Tom Whatley, who made sure this book was carefully guided through the editorial and production process.

About the Author

DR. STEPHEN LEEB is the publisher of newsletters that have a combined readership of 300,000 subscribers and serves as the editor of *The Complete Investor* newsletter, which has earned awards for Editorial Excellence for 2004 and 2005 by the Newsletter & Electronic Publishers Association. As an authority on the stock market, energy trends, and personal finance, Dr. Leeb now believes that within the next few years investors and the world will be struggling with peak energy and peak resources.

Dr. Leeb earned his BS from the University of Pennsylvania's Wharton School of Business in 1968, his MS in math in 1971 from the University of Illinois, and his PhD in psychology from the University of Illinois that same year, earning both higher degrees in just three years—an academic record that still stands.

Dr. Leeb is frequently quoted in the media, including *Investor's Business Daily, USA Today, BusinessWeek*, the *Wall Street Journal*, and the *New York Times*. In addition, Dr. Leeb is a frequent guest on Fox Business, CNN, Bloomberg, Wall Street Journal Radio, and other media outlets.